Insights from Cultural Anthropology

KARL ALLEN KUHN

FORTRESS PRESS
MINNEAPOLIS

INSIGHTS FROM CULTURAL ANTHROPOLOGY

Cover image: Brooklyn Bridge/ Andres Garcia Martin/ Thinkstock & Cruz de Tejeda/ emregologlu/ Thinkstock
Cover design: Rob Dewey

Print ISBN: 978-1-5064-0015-0
eBook ISBN: 978-1-5064-0109-6

For Mary Francis and Eloise,
who bring down the powerful from their thrones
and lift up the lowly

Contents

Series Foreword

"What does this mean?"

That is, perhaps, the most-asked question with regard to the Bible. What does this verse mean? What does this story mean? What does this psalm or letter or prophecy or promise or commandment mean?

The question can arise from a simple desire for information, or the concern may be one of context or relevance: What *did* this mean to its original audience? What *does* it mean for us today?

Someone has said that understanding the Bible is difficult not because meaning is hard to find but because it is so abundant. The problem for interpreters is not *too little meaning* but *too much*. The question becomes, which of all the possible meanings is to be preferred?

But is that really a problem? And, if so, is it not a lovely one?

This abundance of meaning became especially clear in the last decades of the twentieth century when the field of biblical studies embraced dozens of new methods and approaches that had not previously been used or appreciated within the guild. In many ways, biblical studies became more exciting than ever before.

But, yes, the task of understanding the Bible could be daunting. Bible teachers, clergy and lay, who had struggled through college or seminary to learn "the historical-critical method" were suddenly confronted with novel strategies drawn from many other fields of inquiry: sociology, psychology, world religions, cultural anthropology, communication theory, modern literary criticism, and so forth. Then came the avalanche of interpretive approaches grounded in particular philosophical or ideological perspectives: feminism, postmodernism, liberation theology, post-colonialism, queer theology, and on and on.

For the open minded, the yield was an embarrassment of riches. We now understand the Bible in so many different ways: its historical witness, its theological message, its emotional impact, its sociocultural significance, its literary artistry, its capacity for rhetorical engagement, and so on.

At this point in time, we probably understand the Bible better than any who have gone before us. The Bible may challenge us more deeply than it challenged our forebears—and, yet, we have discovered that the Bible also seems to invite us (perhaps to *dare* us) to challenge it back. Many insights into the meaning of Scripture have come from people doing exactly that.

This Insights series from Fortress Press presents brief volumes that describe different ways in which modern scholars approach the Bible, with emphasis on what we have learned from each of these approaches. These are not boring books on esoteric methodology. Some attention, of course, needs to be paid to presumptions and procedures, but the emphasis in each book is on the practical "pay-off" that a given approach has for students and teachers of the Bible. The authors discuss the most important insights they have gained from their approaches, and they provide examples of how those insights play out when working with specific biblical texts in actual real-world circumstances.

Each volume discusses:

- how a particular method, approach, or strategy was first developed and how its application has changed over time;
- what current questions arise from its use;
- what enduring insights it has produced; and
- what questions remain for future scholarship.

Some volumes feature traditional approaches while others focus on new and experimental ones. You will definitely learn things in every book. Your current understanding of "what the Bible means" will be increased. And if you find that the "type of meaning" gained from a particular approach is not what interests you, perhaps you will nevertheless be grateful for the brief tour of a topic that fascinates some of your peers. The books are intentionally brief: they allow us to sample strategies and perspectives, to look down various avenues and see where they lead. They facilitate informed decisions regarding where we might want to go next.

I trust that we are now past the point of arguing over which approach to Scripture is the correct one. Such squabbles were part of the growth pains associated with the guild's aforementioned discovery that meaning is abundant, not so much elusive as ubiquitous.

Those of us who were professors during the late twentieth century sometimes helped our students deal with the methodological confusion by reminding them of the old Indian fable about six blind men and an elephant. In one well-known version of that tale, each of the blind men encounters an elephant and decides "what an elephant is like" based on his singular experience: one feels the trunk and says an elephant is like a hose; another, the tusk and says it is like a spear; another, the ear and says it is like a fan; another, the side and says it is like a wall; another, the leg and says it is like a tree; another, the tail and says it is like a rope. Later, when the men compare notes, each of them insists that he alone understands what an elephant is like: his comrades are totally mistaken.

So, we told our students in the 1990s, each biblical approach or method yields some valid insight into "the meaning of the Bible" (or into "the mystery of divine revelation" or into "what God wants to say to us"). But we would be wise to listen to those whose experience with the Bible is different from ours.

The Insights series is born of humility: its very existence is testimony to our commitment that we need to compare notes about the Bible with openness to each other's diverse perspectives. But, beyond that, I would hope that these volumes might also lead us to admit the limits of our perception. We now see, as the apostle Paul puts it, "in a mirror dimly" (1 Cor 13:12).

Many, including myself, who study the Bible believe it is the word of God, meaning it is a source of divine revelation. For this reason alone, the meaning of the Bible is abundant and ubiquitous. We probably understand the Bible here and now better than any other people in history, and this triumph has brought us to the realization of how little we can understand, now or ever. But, insights? Yes. Those we can claim. Our experiences, our knowledge, and our perspectives do have authenticity and from them we have at least gained some *insights* into the meaning of Scripture. Time to compare notes!

MARK ALLAN POWELL

Preface

I am grateful to Mark Allan Powell, and to Fortress Press, for the invitation to contribute this volume to the Insights series. The writing of this short book has given me the opportunity to take stock of the significant contributions that cultural anthropology has made to my own study of, and appreciation for, Scripture. It has also provided me with a forum for sharing those contributions with others. Indeed, there are practitioners of social-scientific criticism who could have penned a more informed and comprehensive review of the benefits that cultural anthropology provides readers of the Bible. I offer this study not as an expert account but as one "Bible geek's" testimony to how my understanding of the biblical writings and their contexts have been greatly enhanced by the resources cultural anthropology provides. I hope some find this testimony illuminating enough to be drawn to these resources as well.

I am indebted to many practitioners of social-scientific analysis from whom I have learned much over the last twenty years. Their writings and deliberations introduced me to their socially constructed, symbolic, and very useful maps of knowledge. Their passion and generosity drew me in as a fellow fictive kin. Chief among them were my colleagues in the Social-Scientific Task Force of the Catholic Biblical Association, with whom I gathered annually over the course of a decade. While the makeup of this voluntary association shifted over the years, Joan Campbell, Patrick Hartin, Walter F. Taylor Jr., and Ken Stenstrup were constant companions. We gathered under the leadership of two who were among the God-fearing elite in their field: Bruce Malina and John Pilch. We benefited richly from their patronage of knowledge and generosity of spirit. John passed away a year ago, and Bruce a week ago. They are deeply missed.

I am also grateful to several others who assisted in the production of this book. My colleague and friend, Alan Mock, Professor of

Sociology at Lakeland University, has been a frequent conversation part-ner on sociological and anthropological theory. He read through a draft of the manuscript and offered several helpful suggestions that enabled me to refine its analysis. Kim Thimmig, former student and now colleague in ministry, carefully proofed and commented on the draft. James Keller, reference librarian at Lakeland, ably processed scores of interlibrary loan requests from me, making my research much easier from our agrarian setting in rural Wisconsin.

I also give thanks for my ministry of teaching and learning at Lake-land. As a school of the United Church of Christ with an undergraduate program in religion, Lakeland has granted me many opportunities to develop my understanding of Scripture and faith in conversation with my students, colleagues, and members of the wider community. Above all, I give thanks to my family, whose kinship not only shapes my collec-tivist personality in many good and faithful ways but is a source of much blessing and joy.

August 24, 2017

1.

A Socially Sensitive Reading of the Biblical Texts

TAKING AIM AT THE TEXT

Archery is one of my favorite activities. I find it meaningful, challenging, and rewarding. As with most things that require both physical and mental precision, the margin between doing well or not well at all can be rather precarious. Some days, the arrows fly straight and true without exception. I see the target with penetrating clarity, the release is nearly imperceptible, and my eye tracks the arrow effortlessly as it leaves the riser, glides along its parabola path, and slices through its intended mark. I really like those days. But most of the time, the shot and results are mixed, with some arrows finding the mark and others striking waywardly in varying degrees. And then there are those days when very little flies true: the target is fuzzy, I am disconnected from the arrows leaving my bow, and any shot on the mark is more accident than skill.

The discipline of archery can serve as a helpful analogy for the discipline of biblical interpretation. Most who practice it find it meaningful, challenging, and rewarding. We do have those jubilant moments when suddenly the text opens up to us with a blessed clarity and profundity. But most of us also recognize that it doesn't take much to be (way) off the mark when we take a shot at a text. We also realize that perhaps the best we can reasonably hope for most of the time is that our interpretations land in useful proximity to the intended "bull's-eye," whatever that may be. It is no wonder that some consider prayer an important part of the practice of interpretation.

Beyond these points of connection between these two disciplines, there is another. Many archers find it helpful to recite a mantra when they shoot—a phrase or an acronym that helps them follow a consistent set of steps or enter into a frame of mind that facilitates good form. Eventually, if practiced with diligence, the mantra itself becomes such an intimate part of the shot process that its recitation becomes redundant or unconscious—the mantra and the form both become instinctive. This is a goal for which many archers strive. But then, when the shots start missing the mark, the archer can intentionally return to the mantra to reclaim the right state of mind and proper form.

When biblical scholars lay out for themselves and their students basic steps to ensure the proper state of mind and develop "good form" for interpretation, most include "context" as a central element. We are all familiar with the reality that "taking things out of context" often leads to information being misconstrued or misunderstood. In our time and place, arguments between spouses, debates between political candidates, talk-radio shows, and a host of other interactions provide ample examples. Indeed, context is crucial to the reliable transmission of information and meaning in any communicative act. Accordingly, the recognition of the importance of context is also crucial to any interpretive endeavor governed by critical thinking, including biblical interpretation. "Context" belongs in the mantra of any interpreter seeking a useful frame of mind and interpretive form. Otherwise, he or she is just "flinging arrows" at the target, and any good shot is pure accident.

When we talk about context in biblical interpretation, at least three things can be in view. Probably first and foremost, interpreters have in mind the social and historical contexts of the biblical authors or redactors, and their intended recipients. At the same time, many interpreters also find it important to consider their own historical and social contexts and that of other fellow readers of Scripture when discussing the practice and results of biblical interpretation. A third context that significantly impacts the reading of a biblical text and the meaning that is derived from it is the particular set of interpretive assumptions, methods, and objectives that an interpreter practices and pursues.

As an interpreter, when I recite "context" as part of my interpretive mantra, I have all three of these contextual dimensions in view. Each of them is an important part of my exegetical stance. Still, this need not be the case for everyone. For instance, a reader who is only concerned with how the text engages twenty-first-century readers may have little or no interest in the historical and social contexts of the biblical authors, other than an understanding of the biblical language. A hard-core historical critic may believe that her own social and historical context is irrelevant to the task of biblical interpretation since she is engaged in the objective, scientific study of the text, which transcends any scholar's own time and place. And then there are the multitudes of devotional readers who are primarily if not exclusively interested in "what the text means for me and my community"; they give very little thought to these other contexts that shape meaning.

I do not intend to criticize or disparage these other approaches. At the risk of overextending the archery metaphor (as if I haven't already), there are many different kinds of bows that archers use and many different kinds of targets at which they aim. Likewise, most disciplined reading strategies have value, it seems to me. But for those folks who want to aim for the same things I do when lining up in front of a biblical text, for those folks interested in how the biblical texts emerged from and addressed recipients in a certain time and place and who want to pursue a self-aware, critical method for taking a shot at this objective, then insights from cultural anthropology have a lot to offer.

INTRODUCING CULTURAL ANTHROPOLOGY

According to one leading textbook, "anthropology is the study of people—their origins, their development, and contemporary variations wherever and whenever they have been found."[1] Or to quote another, "anthropology is the general study of humans and their ways of life."[2] If you are finding these definitions a bit lacking in specificity, this is understandable. Richley Crapo explains that, "of all the disciplines that study humans, anthropology is by far the broadest in scope." He adds,

> The task that anthropology has set for itself is an enormous one. Anthropologists strive for an understanding of the biological and cultural origins and evolutionary development of the species. They are concerned with all humans, both past and present, as well as their behavior patterns, thought systems, and material possessions. In short, anthropology aims to describe, in the broadest sense, what it means to be human.[3]

As could be expected, then, anthropology consists of several subfields, each of which is itself very broad and further subdivided into different

1. Gary Ferraro and Susan Andreatta, *Cultural Anthropology: An Applied Perspective*, 10th ed. (Stamford, CT: Cengage, 2014), 4.
2. Richley Crapo, *Cultural Anthropology: Understanding Ourselves and Others*, 5th ed. (Boston: McGraw-Hill, 2002), 6.
3. Crapo, *Cultural Anthropology*, 7.

disciplines. *Physical* (or *biological*) *anthropology* studies the development and physical traits of humans as biological organisms. *Archaeology* explores the lifeways of people from the past by excavating and analyzing the material culture they have left behind. *Anthropological linguistics* examines human speech and language as systems of symbolic communication. *Cultural anthropology* (or "social anthropology") consists of the study of specific cultures and the more general, underlying patterns of human culture derived through cultural comparison.[4]

CULTURAL ANTHROPOLOGY: ENGAGING THE SPECIFIC (ETHNOGRAPHY) AND GENERAL (ETHNOLOGY)

The above description of cultural anthropology signals its two primary aims. *Ethnography* is the detailed description of particular cultures in as much detail as possible, usually accomplished through intensive fieldwork, or "participant-observation," in which the anthropologist observes, converses, and even lives with the people under study. The volumes of ethnographies produced by ethnographers provide, then, the resources needed for anthropologists to engage in *ethnology*, the comparative analysis of cultural patterns. For example, by comparing practices of social interaction among persons in different cultures, ethnologists can begin to uncover behavior patterns relative to class distinctions, honor codes, and gender that transcend individual societies. The primary objective of ethnology is to "uncover general cultural principles, that is the 'rules' that govern human behavior."[5]

This dual focus, carefully examining features of specific cultures in order to facilitate cross-cultural comparison, is one of the main differences between the fields of anthropology and sociology. Both fields are broadly labeled as "social sciences." Both rely on some of the same theorists to guide their work, and both share a broad interest in the nature of collective life, and the relations of the individual to the group. But, as helpfully summarized by John Monaghan and Peter Just,

> Anthropology and sociology retain distinct traditions and methods of research. Sociologists are much more likely to focus their research on urban, industrialized societies and they tend to rely on the qualitative analysis of statistical data: the survey is perhaps their most important research tool. Consequently, sociologists are more likely to frame the results of their

---

4. Ferraro and Andreatta, *Cultural Anthropology*, 6–12. See also Robert H. Lavenda and Emily A. Schultz, *Core Concepts in Cultural Anthropology*, 5th ed. (Boston: McGraw-Hill, 2013), 2–10.

5. Ferraro and Andreatta, *Cultural Anthropology*, 12.

research as statements of social causality or correlation, such as linking drug use and homicide rates or unemployment and violent crime. Anthropologists continue to concentrate on exotic societies and rely on participant observation as their chief method and are as concerned with sensitively portraying the texture of daily life as coming up with some universal proposition about social behavior. They are also much more inclined than sociologists to place their findings in the context of a cross-cultural comparison that includes many societies across time and space.[6]

These are, of course, broadly brushed distinctions, and at times the fields of sociology and anthropology overlap and borrow resources from one another. But as a general rule, cultural anthropologists rely on a "close reading" of the daily lives of persons within their environment in order to determine the primary features of their cultures and reflect on what principles of human behavior could be discerned from those observations.

DRIVE TOWARD HOLISTIC ANALYSIS

The extremely broad focus of anthropology in general carries into cultural anthropology as well: nearly every element of human behavior and understanding is fertile ground for analysis. As the discipline has evolved, cultural anthropologists have found it necessary to specialize in particular domains of human culture. For example, some study the ways in which people organize and engage in collective tasks, or how they draw distinctions between themselves, based on kinship, gender, or class. Others focus on expressive and symbolic behavior, such as language, art, music, and ritual. Still others examine material culture, the things people make and use, or how technologies and environments shape each other.[7] Despite this need for specialization, cultural anthropologists frequently engage areas beyond their particular expertise as well as the other subfields of anthropology in order to shape their findings within a wider cultural and methodological context. Their aim is "a comprehensive or holistic view of the human condition."[8]

6. John Monoghan and Peter Just, *Social and Cultural Anthropology: A Very Short Introduction* (Oxford: Oxford University Press, 2000), 73–74.

7. Lavenda and Schultz, *Core Concepts*, 4.

8. Ferraro and Andreatta, *Cultural Anthropology*, 15.

MODELING SOCIAL SYSTEMS, HUMAN PERCEPTION, AND BEHAVIOR

Central to this cross-cultural comparison across time and space is the use of "models." Cultural anthropologists construct hypothesized patterns of human perception and behavior to help them categorize and understand certain sets of expressions and actions in the cultures they study. Ranging from quite simple to complex in detail, these models depict characteristic ways societies function and persons conceive of and respond to their social and physical environments. They serve as heuristic devices that help anthropologists organize and make sense of the data they have uncovered. They also serve as one of the primary resources for discerning and exploring similarities and differences in understanding and behavior across cultures.

Such models come in all shapes and sizes. Macro-level models, or paradigms—seeking to explain the shape and function of human cultures—have proliferated over the last century.[9] Among these, there are three macro-models that have been dominant and serve as a useful introduction to major schools of thought among anthropologists.[10] The *structural-functionalist* model presupposes that every society is a relatively stable and well-integrated system. Nearly every element in that society exists for the purpose of maintaining the status quo. Thus, the various smaller social systems—or institutions—such as family, government, economics, education, and religion operate harmoniously within that society with common values and norms. The natural trend, in this view, is toward stability and cooperation, and change is seen as deviation.

In contrast, the *conflict theory* model views societies as composed of various social groups with competing interests and agendas. Each of these groups utilizes coercive tactics to protect the distinctive interests of its own members. Though at times groups will cooperate with others when it suits their own agendas, constraint and conflict are the norm rather than cooperation and harmony. As a result, according to this view, social structures and institutions trend toward instability and change.

Holding a middle ground of sorts between these two macro-models is a third, the *symbolic model*. This model presupposes that individual and group behavior is organized around the symbolic meanings and expectations attached to objects that are socially valued, such as the self, oth-

9. See Lavenda and Schultz, *Core Concepts*, 217–41.

10. I am indebted here to Bruce Malina's helpful summation of these macro-models in *The New Testament World: Insights from Cultural Anthropology*, 3rd ed. (Louisville: Westminster John Knox, 2001), 19–23.

ers, nature, time, space, and the sacred. The patterns of behavior that characterize interactions between these symbolized agents trend toward both maintaining social equilibrium in ways consistent with shared symbolic meanings and ongoing readjustment in light of new circumstances and situations. In this view, social structures facilitate differentiation and cooperation, constraint and facilitation.

Cultural anthropologists will tend to gravitate toward a particular macro-paradigm and privilege the models associated with it. But many will also draw from various structural-functionalist, conflict, symbolic, and other models in their work. As stated above, models are explanatory tools that vary widely in scope and complexity. A model can be as broad and multilayered as an overview of the political, economic, social, and religious systems of the first-century Roman world, informed by the study of ancient Rome and other advanced agrarian societies with a redistributive economic system. More narrowly, a model can address the political, economic, social, and religious systems of first-century Roman Palestine based on what we can determine about regional developments, Israelite tradition, and the temple cult in particular, and the use of models depicting the function of Roman provinces, the emperor cult, taxation, client kings and aristocracy, lending practices, and slaves and peasants in general. Narrower still, other models explicate typical features of the patron-client relationship between an elite and a member of the lower class, or the reciprocity expected among friends, or the competitive nature of social interaction as embodied in challenge-riposte exchanges. To put it simply, models are simply ways of identifying and organizing social behavior based on what cultural anthropologists have come to understand as typical and recurrent patterns of social life in certain regions and periods.

At the same time, the dialectical relationship between models and data that is common to most scientific disciplines is also characteristic of cultural anthropology. The models serve as hypotheses based on the observation and analysis of multiple cultures. They provide conceptual frameworks for ordering the data under study. And while most models are designed with much care and insight, and have proven useful in multiple contexts, they are also frequently adapted to fit particular contexts better and they are sometimes revised based on new findings.

SENSITIVITY TO ETHNOCENTRISM AND THE
IMPORTANCE OF CULTURAL RELATIVISM

From very early on in its development, the discipline of anthropology has sought to counter our tendency to ethnocentrism by advocating cultural relativism. Ethnocentrism is the very common practice of evaluating an element of someone else's culture from the vantage point of one's own. So, for instance, if you find the consumption of insects (and certain other invertebrates!) disgusting, or the breastfeeding of seven-year-old boys weird, or animal sacrifice troubling, or the Hindu class and caste systems oppressive, or the Inuit practice of leaving infirm parents out in the cold to die heartless, you are likely guilty of ethnocentrism. Now, perhaps there are worse sins one could commit as a human being, but ethnocentrism is a pretty major infraction if you are an anthropologist, *especially* if your personal aversion to certain beliefs and practices gets in the way of your informed, critical analysis. A key ideal governing anthropological study is cultural relativism: any part of a culture under study (idea, thing, or behavior pattern) is to be viewed in relation to its own cultural context, rather than through the norms and value system of the observer's culture. This does not mean that anthropologists are required to abandon or turn off their own value systems in order do their work proficiently. But it does mean that every attempt be made to understand the beliefs and behaviors of the persons under study in relation to their own cultural context, in order to "identify the inherent logic behind certain ideas and customs."[11]

This commitment to "self-aware" analysis has continued to characterize cultural anthropology and evolve within the discipline, especially in response to the postmodern critique. In general, anthropologists have become very sensitive to the reality that all human analysis is ideologically driven and shaped, even in ways that are not always readily apparent. As a result, many among those engaging in ethnographic and ethnologic analyses try to account for how their own cultural contexts and disciplinary commitments shape their observations and interpretation of data. In recent years, some anthropologists have concentrated on studying their own cultures in part to help them better understand how their own social context might influence their interpretation of other cultures.[12] Ethnographers have also begun carefully scrutinizing how their own cultural identity and personal characteristics shape their

11. Malina, *The New Testament World*, 17.
12. Lavenda and Schultz, *Core Concepts*, 5.

contribution to fieldwork interactions and the responses elicited from informants.[13]

CULTURAL ANTHROPOLOGY AND SOCIAL-SCIENTIFIC CRITICISM

A comprehensive introduction to cultural anthropology would address many other characteristic features and tendencies of this very broad discipline. But the pursuit of a holistic purview, the practice of engaging specific contexts drawing from models that pattern human thought and behavior, and the commitment to self-aware analysis—these are the essential features of cultural anthropology that have been most commonly integrated into biblical studies. While insights from cultural anthropology widely pepper various critical readings of the biblical materials, they are engaged most deliberately by scholars practicing what has come to be labeled as "Social-Scientific Criticism." Social-Scientific Criticism refers to "that phase of the exegetical task which analyzes the social and cultural dimensions of the text and its environmental context through the utilization of the perspectives, theories, models, and research of the social sciences."[14] Chief among those social sciences is cultural anthropology.

BRIDGING THE GAP AS MUCH AS POSSIBLE

If one could reduce social-scientific criticism and its use of cultural anthropology to a single aim, it would be to understand with more precision and fullness the social and cultural dimensions of the societies that produced biblical and related writings. For its practitioners, the motivation for doing so can be simply stated: the biblical texts convey meanings derived through a specific culture and particular social arrangements, and these cultures and social arrangements are in many respects very different from our own.[15] The problem these realities pose is that modern readers encounter biblical texts sharing little of the social worlds of those who wrote them. Therefore, if we do not make the attempt to cultivate an anthropologically informed appreciation for the writers of these texts and their contexts, "our Bible reading and subsequent theologizing will

13. Lavenda and Schultz, *Core Concepts*, 12, 234–41.

14. J. H. Elliot, *What Is Social-Scientific Criticism?*, ed. Dan O. Via Jr., Guides to Biblical Scholarship (Minneapolis: Fortress Press, 1993), 7.

15. K. C. Hanson and Douglas E. Oakman, *Palestine in the Time of Jesus: Social Structures and Social Conflicts*, 2nd ed. (Minneapolis: Fortress Press, 1998), 2.

either be noise or our own ideas and values imposed on those authors and their texts."[16]

Most who use cultural anthropology to inform their analysis of biblical and related writings view this practice as an amplification of the historical-critical method. While many practitioners of social-scientific criticism embrace in part the postmodernist critique of positivism, they endeavor to create "adequate bridges for facilitating conversation between the ancient and modern world," as a crucial component of the interpretive process.[17] The text is "analyzed as a vehicle of communication whose genre, structure, content, themes, message, and aim are shaped by the cultural and social forces of the social system and the specific historical setting in which it is produced and to which it constitutes a specific response."[18] This necessitates a holistic and focused engagement of the ecological, geographical, economic, social, political, religious, and other cultural elements shaping the context from which these writings emerged.

MODELING THE ANCIENT WORLD

In addition to recognizing the crucial importance of carefully investigating the social and cultural backdrop of the biblical writings, biblical scholars drawing on cultural anthropology often make use of the models developed by cultural anthropologists or create their own models based on anthropological data. In the next chapter, we will review some of the models that have been commonly and perhaps most fruitfully applied to the biblical writings.

Very few biblical scholars working out of a historical-critical paradigm would question the value of carefully exploring the social and cultural backgrounds of the biblical writings. But practitioners of social-scientific criticism have come under criticism for drawing from cross-cultural models to exegete biblical texts and elucidate their historical contexts. Critics have argued that those utilizing these models sometimes force elements of the text and its background to fit a particular model, and thus end up "templating" texts in ways that obscure rather than clarify their meaning and function. Critics have also questioned the validity of the models themselves, since some tend to be developed, at least in

16. Bruce Malina, *The Social Gospel of Jesus: The Kingdom of God in Mediterranean Perspective* (Minneapolis: Fortress Press, 2001), 13. See also Vernon K. Robbins, "Social-Scientific Criticism and Literary Studies," in *Modelling Early Christianity: Social-Scientific Studies of the New Testament in Its Context*, ed. Philip F. Esler (New York: Routledge, 1995), 277–80.

17. Elliot, *Social-Scientific Criticism*, 59.

18. Elliot, *Social-Scientific Criticism*, 33.

part, with data far removed from the biblical worlds in time and place. In response, practitioners have argued that "the goal of modeling is not to force data into a preconceived mold or pigeonhole," but to work with data in relationship to a hypothetical construct that may prove useful for understanding it.[19] If it becomes clear that the data in view are not adequately explained by the model employed, then the model may be adjusted, modified, or scrapped.[20] Practitioners also point out that the use of models to organize and understand data is not unique to social-scientific criticism, but takes place with all interpretive endeavors whether consciously realized or not.[21] One of the objectives of social-scientific criticism I noted above is the clear and explicit articulation of which models practitioners employ to make sense of the data under review. Practitioners select social-scientific models that they judge to be relevant and relatable to the context of the texts they investigate, and then identify those models for their readers. Such self-awareness and transparency ensure the critical appraisal and value of their analysis. As John Elliot explains,

> All interpreters (including exegetes, historians, and social scientists) can only imagine the social constellations of ancient or alien societies with the help of such models. Only by clarifying, explaining, and justifying one's imaginings or conceptual constructions of social reality can the interpreter expose them to verification and/or critique by others and thereby contribute to an actual advance in understanding.[22]

Two other points may be useful to add in response to the criticism of social-scientific methodology. First, biblical critics have long employed critical tools and models developed in different disciplines and in relation to nonbiblical writings and contexts. The value of a model is less dependent on its provenance than its applicability and usefulness in illuminating certain features of the biblical text. Cross-cultural anthropology is an established discipline that has yielded productive results in analyzing numerous ancient contexts, and it makes sense to try out its methods as we seek to better understand the ancient contexts of the biblical writings. Second, if some practitioners of social-scientific criticism have sometimes been overly zealous in their application of cross-cultural models and have ended up templating the text as a result, that should not surprise

---

19. Hanson and Oakman, *Palestine in the Time of Jesus*, 8.

20. Elliot, *Social-Scientific Criticism*, 44; Hanson and Oakman, *Palestine in the Time of Jesus*, 8.

21. On this point, see Elliot, *Social-Scientific Criticism*, 36–45, and Philip Esler, "Introduction: Models, Context and Kerygma in New Testament Interpretation," in Esler, *Modelling Early Christianity*, 4–5.

22. Elliot, *Social-Scientific Criticism*, 48.

us. For decades now, practitioners of source, form, redaction, rhetorical, ideological, and (fill in the blank) criticism have sometimes done the same! This is not a potential pitfall of social-scientific criticism alone but a problem with the use of any method in any discipline practiced by imperfect, context-laden, perspectival researchers. The arrow only flies as true as the archer, and no archer is perfect.

LOOKING AHEAD

My aim in the following pages is to provide an introduction to some of the tangible benefits cultural anthropology provides readers of biblical texts. The next two chapters will present my "top-ten list" of what I have found to be extremely valuable insights derived from cultural anthropology. Chapter 2 will focus on five political and economic realities of ancient Mediterranean culture, while chapter 3 will turn to five social characteristics (while recognizing that the political, economic, and social features of the biblical words all intertwine). Both chapters will engage several biblical texts in order to illustrate some of the practical, exegetical payoffs of these insights. Chapter 4 will explore the character of biblical writings as "resistance literature" and "conformist literature," drawing from the anthropological concepts of "social movement" and "countermovement." One of the practical benefits these models provide is that they help us recognize the normalcy of competing agendas within Israelite and early Christian communities at moments of crises and pivotal periods of social change. Relatedly, they also help us account for the occurrence of competing perspectives within the biblical writings of both the Israelite and Christian Scriptures. Chapter 5 will take on the challenging topic of purity within the biblical worlds. It will show how models and findings from cultural anthropology and archaeology offer useful resources for addressing several features of Israelite purity concepts and practices, including Jesus's combative interactions with Pharisees in the gospels, that have been difficult for scholars to untangle.

2.

The Political and Economic Tendencies of the Biblical Worlds

My own understanding of biblical literature and the contexts from which it sprung has been significantly enhanced by insights derived from cultural anthropology. I have benefited greatly from the writings of other biblical scholars drawing from this field and time spent with colleagues in the Social Sciences Task Force of the Catholic Biblical Association. Cultural anthropology and the models it provides help us appreciate more fully several crucial dimensions of the worlds that produced the Old and New Testament writings. These next two chapters will highlight ten such essential and extremely valuable insights: this one focusing on political and economic realities, and the next on several social characteristics of the biblical world (though as we shall see, it is really impossible to treat these separately). Overall, the world of the Roman Empire will be our primary touchstone, since we have more detailed information from that era to confirm and guide the anthropological models researchers apply to it. At the same time, I will note how the insights in view are also applicable—though perhaps in a more general, less specific sense—to Old Testament contexts. The chapter will conclude by exploring several texts in order to illustrate the practical exegetical benefits of these insights.

1. RELIGION, POLITICS, ECONOMICS (AND OTHER THINGS) DEFINITELY MIX

At the start, I need to emphasize and celebrate a crucial reality cultural anthropology helps us to see more clearly: for the vast majority of humans throughout history, and for most humans still today, the modes of human thought and activity we label religion, politics, economics, and social relations are really not separable. Rather, they are inextricably intertwined. In a manner consistent with the objectives of cultural anthropology I discussed above, practitioners in this field have helped us to become more aware of how our own cultural tendencies may lead us to overlook crucial dimensions of the ancient contexts we are studying, along with the texts they have produced. In this case, the constant reminders of works informed by cultural anthropology have shifted many away from the erroneous tendency to see the biblical writings as primarily, if not exclusively, *religious* texts.

This is an important insight. The "default mode" of many North Americans—and many North American interpreters of Scripture—is to regard religion as a realm of human thought and activity separate from other social realities, like politics and economics. I think there are at least two reasons for this. On the one hand, many Americans, in trying to embody the Enlightenment ideals of the separation of church and state, or the distinction between scientific reasoning and faith, regard religion as something personal and somewhat private. There are certainly exceptions to this, and I think that religion has become a more prominent part of our public discourse over the last several decades. But many Americans, including American Christians, still tend to segregate religion from their work lives, political engagements, scientific ruminations, and economic practices in varying degrees. The modern proverb, "Religion and politics don't mix!" is a telling instance of this tendency.

Another reason is that many Americans hold to forms of Christianity that assume a sharp contrast between the sacred (having to do with God) and the profane (having to do with material reality). Salvation, the kingdom of God, from this perspective, is more about the hereafter than the here and now. The ultimate goal is to transcend this world to receive God's blessings in the heavenly realm. The current world is temporary, provisional, and of secondary importance to the eternal, spiritual domain of God and the faithful.

As a result, many Americans tend to engage the biblical writings with a *hermeneutic*—a set of assumptions of how they are to be interpreted—that sees them primarily as religious texts providing religious answers to religious questions. When such readers encounter elements of the text that associate God's will, instruction, or announcements of salvation with political, cultural, or economic realities, they tend to spiritualize them into lessons on pride and humility ("He has brought down the powerful from their thrones and lifted up the lowly," Luke 1:52); spiritual hunger ("Blessed are you who are hungry now," Luke 6:21); selfishness ("David saw from the roof a woman bathing; the woman was very beautiful," 2 Sam 11:2); charity ("everything they owned was held in common," Acts 4:32); orderly worship ("I permit no woman to teach or to have authority over a man," 1 Tim 2:12); future, supernatural agents of destruction ("and the beast I saw was like a leopard," Rev 13:2); or the future consummation of the kingdom ("Your kingdom come. Your will be done, on earth as it is in heaven," Matt 6:10). Indeed, these and other biblical passages may have multiple resonances that connect with both "spiritual" and "this-worldly" dimensions of life and faith. But many Americans naturally gravitate to a spiritualized reading that marginalizes if not completely excludes the social, political, or economic dimensions of these passages. When they do so, they are engaging these texts in a fashion that divorces them from their original context and reads them very differently than they were likely heard by their first recipients.

Cultural anthropology simply does not allow us to ignore the down-to-earth resonances sounded by nearly every biblical text. And this is a good thing! Our exegetical arrows fly much truer as a result. By enabling us to become more aware of the interplay between religious, social, political, and economic dimensions of life in the biblical worlds, cultural anthropology helps us get closer to what writers of the biblical texts intended them to convey. Let's turn now to several other critical dimensions of life in the biblical world that cultural anthropology—often in tandem with other disciplines—helps us to explore.

2. THE RICH KEEP GETTING RICHER: THE ROMAN ECONOMY

The world that produced the writings of the New Testament, along with numerous intertestamental traditions and later Israelite and early Christian texts, was the world of Rome. For this reason, it is beneficial for biblical interpreters to be familiar with the tendencies of Roman rule and attending consequences for those living in its vast domain. We also have more data to draw from in assessing the character of the Roman world than we do for the eras that produced most of the writings of the Israelite Scriptures. At the same time, I will be noting how some of these political, social, and economic tendencies and consequences may also be relevant to several Old Testament traditions.

The first-century Mediterranean world was a ruralized society, with most persons—peasants, slaves, tenant farmers—scattered across the landscape in villages and on farms.[1] But while the population was largely rural, power resided in the preindustrial cities, enclaves of the landowning elite. These cities acted as the administrative, religious, and market centers of the villages under their power, enacting elite interests, values, and concerns. Consequently, "the overwhelming majority of persons living in the first-century world (about ninety-eight percent, if not more) would find themselves subject to the demands and sanctions of power-holders outside of their social realm."[2] Borrowing from economic anthropology, a useful model to employ to help us organize the information, we can glean from available sources that the Roman economy was a "redistributive economic system." This system serves to expropriate peasant surplus and redistribute it among those in control.[3] The hierarchical stratification and resource distribution of this system—especially when its social and economic dimensions are combined—could be usefully cast as pyramidal.[4]

At the apex of Roman society was the emperor, father of the empire and its chief patron. To him was due the highest allegiance and honor, and he controlled the resources of the empire. Directly beneath him were other elites, the ruling class, likely comprising no more than 2–3 percent of the population.[5] The elite, themselves divided into several levels, primarily consisted of properly pedigreed families, who were longtime members of the aristocracy and had also established themselves as friends or clients of Roman leaders. The elite would also include a few recent entrants into their ranks, those who through military prowess, political maneuvering, the acquisition of extraordinary wealth, or adoption by an elite family or patron, succeeded in the uncommon achievement

1. Though as Bruce Malina reports in *The New Testament World: Insights from Cultural Anthropology*, 3rd ed. (Louisville: Westminster John Knox, 2001), 84–85, the elite often had two residences, one on the large estates they owned, and another among other elite cloistered in a nodal area of the city.

2. Malina, *New Testament World*, 89.

3. Richard Rohrbaugh, "The Social Location of the Markan Audience," in *The Social World of the New Testament: Insights and Models*, ed. Jerome H. Neyrey and Eric C. Stewart (Peabody, MA: Hendrickson, 2008), 145–46.

4. Though see also the helpful diagram provided by David A. Fiensy in *The Social History of Palestine in the Herodian Period: The Land Is Mine*, Studies in the Bible and Early Christianity 20 (Lewiston, NY: Edwin Mellen, 1991), 158, which uses a vase-shaped image to focus on social stratification.

5. Fiensy, in *Social History of Palestine*, 167, however, estimates that the Palestinian elite comprised only 1 percent of the population.

of joining the elite without being born into this social location. In a continuum from the lower levels of the elite and ranging downward toward non-elite levels were retainers. This included "lower-level military officers, officials and bureaucrats such as clerks and bailiffs, personal retainers, high-ranking household servants, scholars, legal experts, and lower-level lay aristocracy. These worked primarily in the service of the elite and served to mediate both governmental and religious functions to the lower class and to village areas."[6] Retainers also played a crucial role in maintaining the flow of goods and services from producers, primarily the lower classes, to the elite. While a thin slice of the population enjoyed the good fortune of being wealthy merchants (a few of whom managed to join the ranks of the elite), the vast majority of the population were slaves and peasants, including urban merchants, artisans, day laborers, service workers, and rural peasants (those owning and farming small land holdings, tenant farmers, day laborers). Beneath them were those who were viewed by most as outcasts: the dirt poor, diseased or severely handicapped, prostitutes, and other social pariahs.

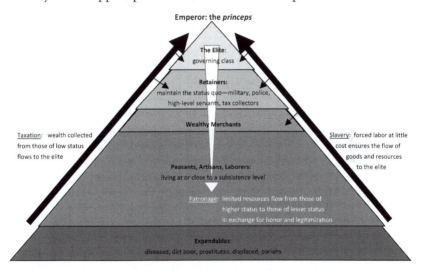

Another key feature of Roman society the preceding diagram seeks to convey is its "redistributive" economic "circulatory system." The lower classes produced nearly all of the goods and services of the empire but retained very little of those resources for its members. Two primary mechanisms were in place to ensure the flow of wealth to the emperor

6. Rohrbaugh, "Social Location," 148.

and the elite: various modes of taxation, and cheap labor in the form of slavery and tenant farming.

Rome heavily taxed its subjects. Scholars estimate that between one-quarter and one-third of the goods harvested or produced by peasants, artisans, and tenant farmers were liquidated into various taxes, tolls, and tithes.[7] Such heavy taxation on the underclass resulted in a precarious existence, with the vast majority of them living slightly above, at, or below a subsistence level. Aggressive taxation also played a significant role in the high rate of debt suffered by peasant farmers. This debt, combined with onerous lending policies and unmercifully high rates of interest established by the elite, resulted in a massive foreclosure of ancestral landholdings throughout the provinces of the empire, including Roman Palestine, in the years leading up to the Common Era.[8]

Still another resource that greatly benefited the elite was their control of relatively cheap labor. Slavery was the engine that drove the economy, as Rome "created an institutionalized system of large-scale dependence on slave labor for the major portion of basic production."[9] Estimates on the number of slaves in the Roman Empire vary among anthropologists, ranging from 25 to 40 percent of the population. But the number of slaves could have easily swelled to the higher end of that range during the years surrounding the Common Era due to Rome's conquest of the Mediterranean (including Palestine) and beyond, augmenting the ranks of those enslaved due to debt.[10] As more and more arable land shifted to the elite, tenant farming, sharecropping, and day labor also became central to agricultural production throughout the empire. Along with many other peasants, these field laborers migrated at or below a subsistence existence, and sharecroppers were in perpetual danger of becoming slaves themselves. Gildas Hamel notes that "especially in the case of sharecropping, the factors of production provided by landowners (land, seeds, traction, tools) were set at a very high rate, usually amounting

7. Gildas Hamel, "Poverty and Charity," in *The Oxford Handbook of Jewish Daily Life in Roman Palestine*, ed. Catherine Hezer (Oxford: Oxford University Press, 2010), 311; Philip A. Harland, "Economy of First-Century Palestine: State of the Scholarly Discussion," in *Handbook of Early Christianity: Social Science Approaches*, ed. Anthony J. Blasi et al. (Walnut Creek, CA: Alta Mira), 521.

8. See Douglas E. Oakman, *Jesus and the Peasants*, Matrix: The Bible in Mediterranean Context (Eugene, OR: Cascade, 2008), 11–22, 137–43; Keith Hopkins, *Conquerors and Slaves*, Sociological Studies in Roman History (Cambridge: Cambridge University Press, 1978), 67. Richard Horsley, *Jesus and the Powers: Conflict, Covenant, and the Hope of the Poor* (Minneapolis: Fortress Press, 2011), 30–31.

9. Richard Horsley, "The Slave Systems of Classical Antiquity and Their Reluctant Recognition by Modern Scholars," *Semeia* 83/84 (1998): 32.

10. Hopkins, in *Conquerors and Slaves*, 9, puts the number at the end of the first century BCE at 35–40 percent.

to half of the total value of the crop, a circumstance which, together with the smallness of the acreage under contract, guaranteed the fall into indebtedness."[11]

In sum, aggressive taxation, an elite-controlled market system that "nickled and dimed" the underclass through rents and tariffs, lending policies that routinely resulted in the foreclosure of peasant landholdings, cheap labor in the form of institutionalized slavery, artisans, and agricultural workers—all this ensured the flow of wealth and resources from the underclass to the elite. This was, as declared by G. E. M. de Ste. Croix, "a massive system of exploitation of the great majority by the ruling class."[12]

3. LIFE WAS (ALL TOO OFTEN) NASTY, BRUTISH, AND SHORT: NON-ELITE LIVING

It is likely that the Roman economy described above yielded consequences that varied regionally due to cultural, geographic, and climatic factors.[13] It is possible that in some circumstances resourceful and fortunate individuals from the underclass could achieve a standard of living that approximated what we might call the "middle class."[14] So, it is not the case that every member of Roman society was either extraordinarily well-heeled or struggling to survive. But according to most researchers, this was the prevailing pattern, and as indicated above, the vast majority of the population lived at the precarious edge of subsistence.

Consequently, in comparison to the vast majority of the population, the elite lived a life of privilege and luxury. While some of the elite may have led busy lives overseeing their estates, managing their business affairs, and enhancing their social contacts, they probably had far more time for pursuing leisure activity and intellectual interests. To be sure,

11. Hamel, "Poverty and Charity," 314.

12. G. E. M. de Ste. Croix, *The Class Struggle in the Ancient Greek World: From the Archaic Age to the Arab Conquests* (Ithaca, NY: Cornell University Press, 1980), 374, cited in Neil Elliott, *The Arrogance of the Nations: Reading Romans in the Shadow of Empire*, Paul in Critical Contexts Series (Minneapolis: Fortress Press, 2008), 7.

13. Some researchers studying the economy of Roman Palestine argue for the recognition of regional variation, including the possibility that due to its fertility, Galilee may have been home to some small and relatively prosperous, family-owned farms. For a helpful review of perspectives, see Alexei Silverstev, "The Household Economy," in Hezer, *The Oxford Handbook of Jewish Daily Life*, 230–44, and Harland, "Economy of First-Century Palestine," 521–25.

14. Jodi Magness, in *Stone and Dung, Oil and Spit: Jewish Daily Life in the Time of Jesus* (Grand Rapids: Eerdmans, 2011), 14, reports on recent studies finding that in some areas of the empire, as high as 20 percent of the population was situated economically between the elite and the lower classes. But she also notes that "the majority of the population still occupied the bottom of the social and economic pyramid. They had little disposable income and lived close to the subsistence level, struggling to maintain a sense of 'wantlessness.'"

the elite were not removed from the vicissitudes of an agonist (competitive) society. They likely encountered repeated challenges to their honor (more on this later). If the elite held positions by appointment, their privileged station could suddenly change due to the whims of those above them. But much more so than the vast majority, the elite avoided deficiencies and situations that dramatically shortened life expectancy. Their access to regular nutrition, superior shelter, rudimentary healthcare and hygiene, and clean(er) water, their avoidance of hard, manual labor, and the protection of cities made it far more likely for them to live into what we call "middle age" than the rest of society.

In sharp—even tragic—contrast, most among the peasant class oscillated near or below a subsistence level. This means that they suffered irregular access to adequate nutrition, water, hygiene, and secure shelter. The consequences of perpetually living on the edge were debilitating.

> For most lower-class people who did make it to adulthood, their health would have been atrocious. By age thirty, the majority suffered from internal parasites, rotting teeth, and bad eyesight. Most had lived with the debilitating results of protein deficiency since childhood. Parasites were especially prevalent, being carried to humans by sheep, goats, and dogs. . . . If infant mortality rates, the age structure of the population, and pathological evidence from skeletal remains can be taken as indicators, malnutrition was a constant threat as well (Fiensy, 1991, 98).[15]

As a result, the life expectancy of the urban peasantry was in the low twenties, and the rural peasantry in the low thirties. Infant mortality rates were about 30 percent, and over half of all peasants living past age one would fail to make it past age sixteen.[16] In short, many of the underclass were struggling to survive, their days filled with worry about the next harvest, the next tax, tribute, rent or loan payment, and often the next meal.

4. HANDOUTS FOR THOSE HUNGRY FOR MORE: PATRONAGE

One may rightly ask how such a system of astounding inequality and dire deprivation could be maintained. Rome's dominant military and police power was one such reason, and perhaps the most decisive. For

15. Rohrbough, "Social Location," 154. The two studies cited by Rohrbough are Joseph Zias, "Death and Disease in Ancient Israel," *Biblical Archaeologist* 54 (1991): 146–59, and Fiensy, *Social History of Palestine.*
16. Rohrbough, "Social Location," 150, 151.

there were those who did resist and found themselves on the wrong end of Roman swords or strung on Roman crosses. But a softer form of social and economic coercion was implemented by the elite through patronage.

Patronage, consisting of a relationship between a patron and clients, was a form of economic redistribution in which some resources were funneled to those of lower status. Returning to the diagram, note the white arrow that descends from the emperor downward. The emperor functioned as the chief patron for the entire empire, as he sanctioned the distribution of wealth to its various members. In turn, the elite would also serve as patrons to elites of lesser status and sometimes even to members of lower classes, and this would continue on down the social scale. What patrons offered their clients varied: financial and/or legal assistance during times of crisis, protection from enemies, food, gifts, mentoring, appointments to an official post, among other favors or forms of assistance. In return, the patron could expect to receive honor, information, and political support from clients.[17] Often, the relationship and exchanges between patron and client were face-to-face; at times favors and requests were mediated through an intermediary, or "broker." What the patron-client system amounted to for the peasantry was—to use a modern analogy—a rather meager form of "trickle down" economics. It functioned as the means by which elites could increase honor and status, acquire and hold office, achieve power and influence, and increase wealth. In other words, it kept the social hierarchy intact.[18]

As the downward arrow indicates in the diagram, the dispersal of wealth lessened the further patronage went down the social scale. Through patronage, the greatest resources were disbursed to those already at or near the level of elite. For peasants, the resources received through patronage could be of significant temporary assistance but did not fundamentally alter their social and economic station. To put it differently, patronage among the upper classes was about favors, networking, and advancement. Patronage for the peasantry was about gaining resources that eased in varying degrees their struggle to stay out of insurmountable debt and even survive. To put it more crassly, it simply took a lot less to buy the allegiance of a peasant than a fellow elite.

Within Roman Palestine, elite who offered patronage to the underclass in order to gain their compliance or support included the temple establishment. The temple was the center of the Judean economy. It received tithes, offerings, and sacrifices from the populace, and also col-

17. Hanson and Oakman, *Palestine in the Time of Jesus*, 65.
18. Hanson and Oakman, *Palestine in the Time of Jesus*, 66.

lected tribute for Rome, in exchange for its "brokerage" of divine forgiveness and blessing.[19] The economic benefits for the priesthood were significant, and members of the priestly aristocracy had acquired much of the arable land in the region through the onerous lending policies and peasant foreclosure we discussed in the preceding section.[20] When it came to dealing with tenants and debtors, the priestly elite were expected to be just and kind to their tenants. But "they could also use the threat of short-term leases, eviction and physical violence (prison and torture)."[21] According to some Israelite sources, the priestly elites often opted for the latter: "Josephus and later rabbinic writings report the high priest's predatory practices of sending armed thugs and goon squads to the village threshing floors to seize the tithes intended for the ordinary priests and to intimidate the peasants in other ways (*Ant.* 20.9.2 §§206–7)."[22] While the temple establishment did collect offerings for the poor, it appears that the success of those offerings was inconsistent and the sums raised were dwarfed by the amounts set aside for personnel and the cult. As indicated by textual and archaeological evidence, more substantial and consistent assistance was provided to the poor on a community level and administered through synagogues. Synagogues served as hostels for transients and displaced peoples, and funds were established for both long-term and emergency relief.[23] But this community-based assistance is probably best understood as outside of the practice of patronage.

5. THERE IS ONLY SO MUCH TO GO AROUND: LIMITED GOOD

The mindset driving and reinforced by this "massive system of exploitation of the great majority by the ruling class" was one of scarcity, what anthropologists refer to as the perception of "limited good" commonly found in similar economic and social systems.

> Thus extensive areas of behavior are patterned in such a way as to suggest to one and all that in society as well as in nature—the total environment—all the desired things in life, such as land, wealth, prestige, blood, health, semen, friendship and love, manliness, honor, respect and status, power and influ-

19. Horsley, *Jesus and the Powers*, 7.
20. Hamel, "Poverty and Charity," 314.
21. Hamel, "Poverty and Charity," 314
22. Horsley, *Jesus and the Powers*, 76–77.
23. Hamel, "Poverty and Charity," 320.

ence, security and safety—literally all goods in life—exist in finite, limited quantity and are always in short supply.[24]

Simply put, limited good is the widely held axiom that there is only so much of all good things to go around, and it is never enough. Life is a zero-sum game. If you have more, then I have less. Hence, any apparent relative improvement in someone's access to resources or social position within a community may be viewed by others as a threat to the entire community, for it could upset the delicate balance of resources that had been achieved. Even more worrisome, it could result in even fewer resources for those already clinging to the precarious edge of subsistence. Imagine, if you will, two children dividing up a cherished piece of cake (but your half is bigger!). More relevant still, consider farmers in the southwest United States wrangling over water rights, or persons struggling to get healthcare services in developing (and some "first-world") countries. Access to these scarce resources, even today, could mean the difference between farms, and human bodies, that flourish or fail.

SEEING THESE INSIGHTS IN ACTION

As mentioned previously, the insights provided by cultural anthropology do not constitute, on their own, an interpretive method. Rather, when at their most useful, they refine the aim of interpreters to make sense of the biblical texts within their own social and historical contexts. Below, I briefly explore four texts in order to illustrate how the five insights we have just reviewed can refine our interpretive endeavors.

MARY'S MAGNIFICAT (LUKE 1:46–55)

Our first stop is Mary's song of praise in Luke's infancy narrative. As you prepare to read it, please try to keep first and foremost in your mind the insights we have just reviewed. Recall especially the intertwining of religious, economic, and political realms of life, and the redistributive economic system of the Roman world, with its beneficial consequences for the elite, and its dire consequences for nearly everyone else. Note, too, other features of the first-century world that are also in play, such as the long-standing Israelite hope—held in various forms—that God would one day return to reclaim God's creation from the godless and to restore

---

24. Malina, *New Testament World*, 89.

the fortunes of the faithful (what most Israelites meant when they talked about the awaited "kingdom of God").

> And Mary said,
> "My soul magnifies the Lord,
>   and my spirit rejoices in God my Savior,
> for he has looked with favor on the lowliness of his servant.
>   Surely, from now on all generations will call me blessed;
> for the Mighty One has done great things for me,
>   and holy is his name.
> His mercy is for those who fear him
>   from generation to generation.
> He has shown strength with his arm;
>   he has scattered the proud in the thoughts of their hearts.
> He has brought down the powerful from their thrones,
>   and lifted up the lowly;
> he has filled the hungry with good things,
>   and sent the rich away empty.
> He has helped his servant Israel,
>   in remembrance of his mercy,
> according to the promise he made to our ancestors,
>   to Abraham and to his descendants forever."

Now that you have reflected on the passage, consider this attempt to explain how Mary's song of praise in Luke's infancy narrative is best understood by its recipients today:

> Mary says that God reverses the strengths of this world. Those who are mighty are "pulled down." Those who are lowly are exalted. Those who are hungry are filled with good things, while the rich are "sent away empty." This is another way to describe salvation by grace. God does not save those who are already strong and powerful. In fact, He saves those who are weak, those who know that they are in need.
> The Magnificat also reminds us to beware of worldly riches and power. At the same time our God is exalting the lowly, He is pulling down the mighty. He humbles the proud, and He does this by bringing them down. If you are rich, the gospels tell us that you will have a hard time entering the kingdom. You will have a hard time acknowledging your need. You will have a hard time being hungry. And so beware anything that makes you feel strong and self-sufficient. Be vigilant to keep a posture of spiritual dependency. That sounds strange, but you have to work to remind yourself that you need God. Do not become complacent in your routine, thinking that you have it figured out. Practice humility.[25]

25. Steven Wedgeworth, "The Meaning of the Magnificat," *Wedgeword* (blog), December 14, 2014, https://tinyurl.com/ycrmm74p.

While this reading acknowledges the economic references in the passage, it treats those references to poverty and wealth on a largely metaphorical level. The rich are those who think that they are strong and powerful, the proud who fail to recognize their dependence on God: "If you are rich . . . [y]ou will have a hard time acknowledging your need. You will have a hard time being hungry." The lowly are those who recognize that they need God, the humble that God will save by grace: "Be vigilant to keep a posture of spiritual dependency."

In my experience, this is a very common reading of the passage by North American Christians. It is also reflected in our hymnody based on the Magnificat.[26] But would this largely "spiritualized" and "individualized" reading be common among its recipients in the first-century Roman world? Did Luke scribe this song as a lesson on humility and pride for individual believers as it is so often understood by readers today? Or, did Luke intend it to be a harbinger of the world-upending arrival of the kingdom of God, overturning the elite-sanctioned yet desperate inequity and suffering experienced by so many, as promised by the father of Israel those many years ago? Which reading is closer to the mark, making better sense of Luke's social, political, and religious contexts? Scholars informed by the five insights offered above typically conclude that Mary's song is a bold declaration that with the arrival of God's messiah, the evils of the present age—including widespread sociopolitical marginalization and economic deprivation—shall be overcome.

Broadening our purview, we find that numerous features of Luke's full two-volume account echo the social, political, and economic reversal announced here near its start by Mary. Throughout his narrative Luke is calling for individuals to welcome the arrival of God's kingdom and the Lord Jesus, and no longer align themselves with Rome, the lord Caesar, or any of his underlings (e.g., Luke 4:1–14; Acts 4:8–12). The hoarding of resources, the lack of hospitality toward those in need, the greed and self-superiority of the elite—these elemental parts of the Roman economic and social systems—are simply evil (e.g., Luke 6:24–26; 10:29–37; 11:37–52; Acts 12:20–23). In sharp contrast, those who seek to be Jesus's disciples are to start living *now* as if the kingdom of God were already among them, which it is (e.g., Luke 17:20–22; 18:1–14; Acts 2:14–36). The rich are to give up their possessions, selling all for the sake of the poor or the ministry of the church. Resources are to be distributed according to need, not social rank (e.g., Acts 2:43–47; 4:32–37; see also 5:1–11!). Flesh-and-blood authorities are to be resisted when they seek

26. David Neff, "Misreading the Magnificat," *Christianity Today*, December 20, 2012, https://tinyurl.com/y78znyff.

to defy the reign of God and God's Messiah (e.g., Acts 4:23–31). In short, just as Jesus inaugurated the arrival of God's long-awaited reign in his life, death, and resurrection, so now is the church to take up Jesus's ministry and embody the new world God is fashioning into being. The very real social and economic reversal that Mary announces as having begun in the conception of her child is to continue in the ministry of his followers as they await the kingdom's full consummation.[27]

MARK 11:15–19

Markan scholars informed by these insights from cultural anthropology similarly conclude that one of Mark's main objectives was to challenge elite aims and the social and economic oppression perpetuated by Rome. Many have noted that Mark's narrative presents a contrast between two sets of values, two contrasting orientations to life: what God wills for people, and what people will for themselves. Human sinfulness is reflected in the fact that people are self-oriented and self-serving. This becomes strikingly clear in the narrative and dialogue surrounding Jesus's three passion predictions (8:22–10:52): "people want to 'save their lives' (8:35), to 'acquire the world' (8:36), to 'be great' (9:35), and to 'exert authority over' or to 'lord over' people (10:43–44)."[28] In response to the disciples who frequently articulate the quest for self-preservation and gratification, Jesus explains "the values of the rule of God that underlie his actions and teachings."[29]

For Mark, it therefore follows that wealth is also an obstacle to entering the realm of God's rule. The pursuit and maintenance of wealth, especially in the agonistic, hierarchical world of Rome, is a quest for power, self-preservation, and gratification. It is an orientation, a deficiency of will and spirit, that even near-perfect allegiance to Torah cannot overcome (see 4:18–19; 10:17–27).

The fear of loss—loss of status, privilege, and even life—and the quest for blessing in all the wrong places, is also reflected in the evangelist's depiction of the social elite. The misalignment of their value system is repeatedly unmasked and attacked by Jesus. The elites' effort to main-

---

27. For a more extensive review of the major rhetorical impulses of Luke's two-volume account, see Karl Kuhn, *The Kingdom according to Luke and Acts* (Grand Rapids: Baker Academic, 2015), 203–74. See also Halvor Moxnes, *The Economy of the Kingdom: Social Conflict and Economic Relations in Luke's Gospel* (Eugene, OR: Wipf & Stock, 1988).

28. David Rhoads, "Losing Life for Others in the Face of Death: Mark's Standards of Judgment," in *Gospel Interpretation: Narrative Critical & Social Scientific Approaches*, ed. Jack Dean Kingsbury (Harrisburg, PA: Trinity Press International, 1997), 85.

29. Rhoads, "Losing Life for Others," 84.

tain power and status is motivated by fear. Herod fears John the Baptist (6:20) but not more than he fears being shamed by his guests (6:26). Pilate fears the crowd and so hands Jesus over to be flogged and crucified (15:15). The Israelite leaders fear having their status compromised by this itinerant healer and preacher, who challenges their system of piety (Mark 3:1–6; 7:1–23), the propriety of the temple cult (11:15–19), and their pursuit of wealth and honor (7:1–13). Thus, already by 3:6, alliances are forged among the elite in opposition to their common enemy: "The Pharisees went out and immediately conspired with the Herodians against him, how to destroy him" (3:6; see also 11:18; 12:13; 14:43).

It is within this narrative context—a context in which the elite pursuit of wealth and oppression of others is repeatedly undermined by Jesus's teaching and ministry—that the well-known story of Jesus cleansing the temple must be understood.

> [15] Then they came to Jerusalem. And he entered the Temple and began to drive out those who were selling and those who were buying in the Temple, and he overturned the tables of the money changers and the seats of those who sold doves; [16] and he would not allow anyone to carry anything through the Temple.
> [17] He was teaching and saying, "Is it not written,
> 'My house shall be called a house of prayer for all the nations'?
> But you have made it a den of robbers."
> [18] And when the chief priests and the scribes heard it, they kept looking for a way to kill him; for they were afraid of him, because the whole crowd was spellbound by his teaching. [19] And when evening came, Jesus and his disciples went out of the city.

Thus, the question that the tendencies of Mark's narrative lead us to ask is the following: In what way has God's temple been turned by the "chief priests and scribes" into a "den of robbers," as Jesus announces (v. 17)? How has the temple come to represent elite greed and oppression? Building on the five insights offered above, consider these additional religious, political, and economic realities of Jesus's time.

As we noted above, the priestly aristocracy (Sadducees) drew from their sacred tradition regulating the maintenance of the temple cult in order to shape that institution into a major source of political and economic capital. Sacred tradition circumscribed access to the temple via purity laws and also empowered certain persons to administer its benefits of cleansing and atonement. Yet these ministrations came with a price. The Sadducees used these sacred traditions as a means of legitimating their control of the temple cult, which—along with their more-often-than-not cozy alliance with the Herodians—eventually resulted in their control of a large share of the economic and judicial system of Judea. In this passage, by overturning the tables of the money-changers and the seats of the dove-sellers (the sacrificial animal most likely to be purchased by the poor), Jesus is likely targeting and condemning, in symbolic fashion, two oppressive realities overseen and contrived by the temple elite.

First, the mandatory, annual temple tax provided a lucrative revenue stream for the priests. Beyond the required amount of the tax, worshippers were also required to remit the tax in Tyrian shekels, for which there was an additional exchange rate that would have added to the struggle of the poor majority to pay the tax.[30] As we also noted above, taxation further gave the Israelite elite—including high-level priests—a mechanism for ensuring widespread peasant indebtedness and access to peasant landholdings that were routinely foreclosed: landowning farmers got behind in their tax payments, borrowed against their land in order to make those payments, and then many lost their land when they couldn't pay back the loans. This added loan interest and land rent to elite priests' incomes and gave them access to cheap labor in the form of tenant farmers, sharecroppers, and slaves.[31]

Second, peasant land foreclosure also—and here is why the selling of animals in the temple precincts was targeted by Jesus—gave the elite a virtual monopoly on the sacrificial animal trade. What was once an important source of revenue for area farmers working their ancestral landholdings became, through peasant indebtedness due to high taxes and land foreclosure due to obscenely high rates of interest, yet another source of revenue for the temple elite and their fellow aristocrats. The selling of sacrificial animal to worshippers and pilgrims within the temple precincts in the days leading up to Passover was not the problem. The problem was that commerce now represented one more way in which the temple elite were complicit in the widespread oppression and desperation imposed on the many by a select few who controlled the religious, political, and economic levers of empire. Karen J. Wenell helpfully summarizes Jesus's engagement with the Sadducees and assortment of other elite in this section of Mark:

> Wealth is a primary value associated with the opponents of Jesus in the Temple conflict scenes in Mark 11–12. The robbers (lēstai) of 11:17 have, in a sense, stolen what belongs to God (12:13–17) and opposed his son (12:1–10). Jesus protests the values of power and wealth connected to the

---

30. Magness, *Stone and Dung*, 101–2.
31. See Douglas E. Oakman, "Cursing Fig Trees and Robbers' Dens: Pronouncement Stories within Social-Systemic Perspective: Mark 11:12–15 and Parallels," *Semeia* 64 (1993): 260.

central Temple which conflict with God's dominion and care for the least in society, such as the poor widow.[32]

Jesus's action in the temple unmasks and challenges the temple elite's quest for control and perversion of God's house through their greed and neglect of neighbor. They are robbing the people they are called to serve. Subsequent conflicts in this section of Mark further emphasize the temple elite's obduracy (11:27–33; 12:18–27), rejection of God's reign (12:1–12), collusion with Caesar (12:13–17), and quest for status and wealth while devouring others (12:38–44).

REVELATION 18:1–24

Our third stop will be the imaginative, engaging, somewhat confusing, and variously understood book of Revelation. Let me begin with a few comments about Revelation in general. As a work belonging to the genre of *apocalyptic*, the writing offers a revelation (*apocalypsis*) received from the heavenly realms of events that are going to unfold leading up to the consummation of God's kingdom, including the overthrow of all evil and deliverance of the faithful. While it is clear that the book has a future orientation, scholars generally discern that most of the personages (including beasts!) and events it portrays in metaphorical guise are referring to incidents and persons that are part of the writer's immediate historical context in the first century. In contrast, most popular-level uses of Revelation interpret nearly all of its imagery as referring to matters that have yet to take place. This is sometimes called a "prophetic" approach to Revelation. The "historical" approach favored by most scholars, however, tries to figure out how much of Revelation's fantastic imagery is related to realities of the Roman world. This is the approach I will employ below, and one that the insights of cultural anthropology can enhance.

The passage we are going to address occurs in the section of the work, spanning chapters 18–20, in which the defeat of evil in its various forms unfolds toward its climax and conclusion. In 18:1–24, an angel proclaims the fall of Babylon, that historic enemy of God's people, Israel.

Due to its length, I will not cite all of 18:1–24, but here is a portion that is somewhat representative of the whole:

32. Karen J. Wenell, "Contested Temple Space and Visionary Kingdom Space in Mark 11–12," *BibInt* 15 (2007): 332.

^{1} After this I saw another angel coming down from heaven, having great authority; and the earth was made bright with his splendor. ^{2} He called out with a mighty voice,

"Fallen, fallen is Babylon the great!
It has become a dwelling-place of demons,
a haunt of every foul spirit,
a haunt of every foul bird,
a haunt of every foul and hateful beast.
^{3} For all the nations have drunk
of the wine of the wrath of her fornication,
and the kings of the earth have committed fornication with her,
and the merchants of the earth have grown
rich from the power of her luxury."
^{4} Then I heard another voice from heaven saying,
"Come out of her, my people,
so that you do not take part in her sins,
and so that you do not share in her plagues;
^{5} for her sins are heaped high as heaven,
and God has remembered her iniquities.
^{6} Render to her as she herself has rendered,
and repay her double for her deeds;
mix a double draught for her in the cup she mixed.
^{7} As she glorified herself and lived luxuriously,
so give her a like measure of torment and grief.
Since in her heart she says,
"I rule as a queen;
I am no widow,
and I will never see grief,"
^{8} therefore her plagues will come in a single day—
pestilence and mourning and famine—
and she will be burned with fire;
for mighty is the Lord God who judges her." (18:1–8)

These are scathing words of judgment! Babylon the great has fallen. And deservedly so, for "her sins are heaped as high as heaven." But who or what is Babylon?

On one level, Babylon is the historic enemy of God's people, the nation-state responsible for the calamitous destruction of Israel (Judah) in 587 BCE. Israel was a vassal of the Babylonian empire, but twice within a dozen years two kings of Israel rebelled against their overlords to the north (see 2 Kings 24). After the second rebellion, Babylon had enough of this recalcitrant nation defying its will. Babylon's armies invaded, killed thousands, leveled the city of Jerusalem and its walls, and razed

the temple. Then, Nebuchadnezzar had the survivors exiled into Babylon. Babylon effectively erased Israel as a sociopolitical entity. And nearly
all that defined Israel as a people—land, temple, king—was gone. For
most Israelites, even though the Babylonian invasion was an act of God's
judgment against Israel because of Israel's faithlessness, Babylon still represented an arrogant, destructive, and evil people who deserve God's
retributive wrath. For a bitter taste of Israelite antipathy for Babylon,
consider Psalm 137.

> O daughter Babylon, you devastator!
> Happy shall they be who pay you back what you have done to us!
> Happy shall they be who take your little ones and dash them against the
> rock! (137:8)

By the time John is recording his visions, however, the Babylonian
empire that (almost) destroyed Israel was long gone. But in the minds of
many Israelites in this day, including Israelite Christians, there is another
power equally as terrible as Babylon the Devastator threatening all that
is good within the world. Satan has a new regime under his command,
casting creation into another era of darkness: Rome.[33]

Knowing what we do about life in first-century Rome helps us to better understand and appreciate the iniquities John's vision associates with
the empire. Here Rome is cast as an alluring seductress committing fornication with (or, perhaps raping) the realms under her command, and
offering wealth to those who support her quest for dominance and luxury (v. 3). Much of the language describing Rome's iniquitous ways is
rather generalized and sexualized, reflecting the prophetic tendency to
describe idolatry as sexual infidelity (see, e.g., Ezek 16:1–58; Hos 1). At
the same time, we can also discern that the crimes for which Rome shall
be judged center on the economic and political exploitation of others.
Rome has "glorified herself and lived luxuriously," elevating herself as
queen of creation (v. 7). Merchants who counted on Rome's insatiable
drive for material pleasure as their own avenue to wealth will mourn her
sudden and calamitous fall (vv. 11–19). Rome will be rendered what its
drive for wealth and power has rendered others: "torment and grief" (vv.
6–7). For Rome's trade has included not only the dainties and niceties
that its elite crave but also "human bodies and souls" (v. 13).

Thus, what our insights about the economic and political realities of
the Roman world help us appreciate as we consider this passage from

33. Most scholars understand the first beast in Revelation 13 as a depiction of either the
Roman emperor Nero or Domitian, and the second beast as a reference to the imperial cult
promoting the worship of deified emperors.

Revelation is that first-century Christians understood the political and economic oppression perpetrated by Rome—the source of so much suffering for so many—as nothing short of demonic. The Roman emperor rules not with a divine mandate, as Rome often claims, but a satanic mandate. Through the rhetorically charged language of apocalyptic, John (like Luke and Mark) is urging his fellow believers to see the truth of what truly empowers Rome and the falsehood of its claims to mastery. Don't take for your own the ways of Rome! Do not fall to the lies she speaks or the traps she lays. Do not become complicit in her crimes (v. 4). But rejoice that her days are numbered and that her murderous ways, and her war against the righteous, shall come to an end (vv. 20–24).

MICAH 2:1–11

The prophet Micah prophesied during a pivotal and tragic period in Israel's history. His ministry began during the last years of the divided nation—a 200-year period beginning after the reign of Solomon in 922 BCE when Israel was divided into the Northern and Southern Kingdoms and lasting until the fall of the Northern Kingdom to Assyria in 722. Thus, Micah witnessed the final, desperate days of the Northern Kingdom (often referred to as "Israel") and the ongoing threat Assyria posed for the Southern Kingdom, Judah. While Judah survived its own Assyrian siege at the hands of Sennacherib in 701, Micah predicted that Jerusalem would eventually fall as an act of God's judgment, because the people had been unfaithful to the covenant promises (see 3:1–12). Chief among these violations of the covenant identified by Micah have been the neglect and abuse of the poor by the leaders of Israel.

¹ Alas for those who devise wickedness
    and evil deeds on their beds!
When the morning dawns, they perform it,
    because it is in their power.
² They covet fields, and seize them;
    houses, and take them away;
they oppress householder and house,
    people and their inheritance.
³ Therefore, thus says the LORD:
Now, I am devising against this family an evil
    from which you cannot remove your necks;
and you shall not walk haughtily,
    for it will be an evil time.
⁴ On that day they shall take up a taunt-song against you,

and wail with bitter lamentation,
and say, "We are utterly ruined;
    the LORD alters the inheritance of my people;
how he removes it from me!
    Among our captors he parcels out our fields."
5 Therefore you will have no one to cast the line by lot
    in the assembly of the LORD.
6 "Do not preach"—thus they preach—
    "one should not preach of such things;
    disgrace will not overtake us."
7 Should this be said, O house of Jacob?
    Is the LORD's patience exhausted?
    Are these his doings?
Do not my words do good
    to one who walks uprightly?
8 But you rise up against my people as an enemy;
    you strip the robe from the peaceful,
from those who pass by trustingly
    with no thought of war.
9 The women of my people you drive out
    from their pleasant houses;
from their young children you take away
    my glory forever.
10 Arise and go;
    for this is no place to rest,
because of uncleanness that destroys
    with a grievous destruction.
11 If someone were to go about uttering empty falsehoods,
    saying, "I will preach to you of wine and strong drink,"
    such a one would be the preacher for this people! (2:1–11)

The powerful and polyphonic imagery in this passage is far richer than we can unpack here. But for a start, let's zero in on verses 1–5. Verse 1 introduces to us the actors in view and the prophet's characterization of their actions. These are people who lie awake at night, devising "wickedness" and "evil deeds"! And, unfortunately, these folks have the power to perform this wickedness when morning dawns. They are people of means and position.

As the passage unfolds, we learn more specifics about the evil machinations of these late-night schemers. They greedily covet the fields and homes of others and now plot to seize them. They oppress householder and house and take away their ancestral inheritance (v. 2). Similarly, they drive out women from their homes and undermine the witness of ancestral landholdings to God's blessing and glory for future generations (v. 9).

We don't have as much information about the economic system of eighth-century BCE Israel as we do for first-century Rome. Thus, the models we relied on above to describe the Roman economy are of less help to us here. We are also unsure of the specific mechanisms these evil persons employed to "seize" and "take away" the property of other Israelites. This wording (along with "covet") surely reminds its hearers of the notorious royal couple, Ahab and Jezebel, who murdered Naboth and seized his ancestral land (1 Kings 21). But the specific policies and practices that facilitated the land-grabbing condemned by Micah are unclear to us. At the same time, the crucial insight reinforced by cultural anthropology that must guide our analysis of this passage also is the intertwining of religious, social, political, and economic realities in the ancient world. Accompanying that insight is the well-established reality from the study of agrarian economies that those with political power and social standing often utilized their position to extract resources from those under their control.

These realities—ones that cultural anthropology helps us appreciate—can guide and reinforce our understanding of the passage. First, they add further support to the discernment of many interpreters that the late-night schemers are members of the elite. The allusion to Ahab and Jezebel, the specific reference to "heads of Jacob" and "rulers of the house of Israel" and their extreme perversions of justice in 3:1–3, lead most commentators to conclude that the seizure of landholdings identified in 2:1–11 is the result not of tribal warfare or peasant uprising but of elite oppression. The model of an agrarian economy that includes peasant loss of land due to the economic policies established by the elite provides a realistic and commonly occurring scenario by which to make sense of 2:1–11.

Second, we also know from cultural anthropology that elites often claim a divine mandate to rule, along with elevated or inspired insight into the will of the divine (more on this in the next chapter). In this oracle, Micah announces that the elite's seizure of other Israelites' land will be met with Yahweh's wrath. The "family" that is perpetuating this evil will in turn face it themselves (v. 3). Their power and position will fail them, and their ancestral landholdings will be parceled out among their captors (v. 4). But the elite claim to know better the will of Yahweh and dismiss the warnings of doom sounded by the prophets. "Don't preach this!" the elite cry. "This won't happen to us!" (v. 6). Instead, they prefer prophets who simply reinforce their profligate pursuits: "Party On, Man!" (v. 11).

Finally, these insights also help attune us to the important observation that the economy and social stability idealized and defended by the eighth-century prophets revolved around a specialized form of land ownership that was designed to limit elite control while facilitating peasant prosperity and stability. For Israel, the land belonged to Yahweh (see Lev 25:23). As Yahweh stipulates in Joshua 14–21, land was distributed by each tribe into ancestral landholdings, and laws were developed to protect those landholdings from loss due to scheming, abusive rulers and even debt (Exod 22:25–27; Lev 25:25–54). As Delbert Hillers notes, the actions of those whom Micah condemns were "an assault on the basic structure of the people of God." He goes on to state,

> The economic and social ideal of ancient Israel was of a nation of free land-holders—not debt-slaves, sharecroppers, or hired workers—secure in possession, as a grant from Yahweh, of enough land to keep their families. "Each under his own vine and his own fig tree" summarizes the ideal. Other ideals, such as justice, mutual love and fidelity, a close-knit family, and so on, depend on the achievement of this sort of economic security. If the family land was lost, little other economic opportunity remained.[34]

This helps us understand why Micah and other eighth-century prophets such as Isaiah and Amos targeted land forfeiture as an especially egregious form of social and economic oppression, *and* a heinous violation of Israel's covenant with Yahweh. In their view, without this basic economic structure in place, Israel simply cannot live in accord with Yahweh's designs for Israel: "from their young children you take away my glory (or blessings) forever!" (v. 9). Without it, Israel cannot stand: "Arise and go, for this is no place to rest, because of uncleanness that destroys with grievous destruction" (v. 10).

---

34. Delbert R. Hillers, *Micah: A Commentary on the Book of the Prophet Micah*, Hermeneia (Minneapolis: Fortress Press, 1988), 33. I was led to Hillers's comment by Daniel J. Simundson, *The Book of Micah*, NIB 7 (Nashville: Abingdon, 1996), 550.

3.

The Social Tendencies of the Biblical Worlds

In this chapter, we continue our review of ten valuable insights into the biblical worlds provided or enhanced by cultural anthropology. The five addressed in the previous chapter focused on economic and political dimensions of those worlds. Here we will explore five additional cultural traits revolving around social relations. But as we shall continue to see, these social dynamics intersect with the political and economic matters already discussed. Remember, these elements of the biblical worlds are all interconnected! As in the previous chapter, we will again briefly explore several texts in order to illustrate the practical exegetical benefits of these insights.

1. REAL MEN RULE: PATRIARCHY

Throughout much of the Mediterranean region during the biblical era, idealized conceptions of humanity were overwhelmingly male. Maleness was the standard, perhaps even the baseline, for defining human. The Israelite Scriptures reflect the idealization of maleness in a myriad of ways, including the highly imbalanced attention they give to male characters in their narratives, the overtly patriarchal character of laws governing the household, property, cult, and sexuality, and the masculinization of God. While there are some female characters, even heroes, remembered and celebrated in Israel's sacred traditions (e.g., Hagar, Sarah, Rebekah, Tamar, Hebrew midwives, Miriam, Zipporah, Deborah, Ruth, Dinah, Esther, Judith), even their stories underscore the inescapable reality that the world of ancient Israel was a man's world (case in point: recall the interview protocol for Esther's bid to become queen).

This was no less the case for the realms of Greece and Rome, in which the glorification of the masculine (and denigration of the feminine) was elemental to their respective cultures. At the same time, while maleness was the ideal in the Greco-Roman world, according to the elite and their retinues, very few men ably reflected that ideal. There were men, and then there were "unmanly men."[1] In sum, real men ruled, and they exercised that rule in four areas of social life. They ruled sexually, utilizing the power of their phallus to penetrate others. They ruled over their families, exercising their paternal power to control the finances, inheritance, marriage, and social relations of their wives, children, and slaves. They ruled politically, governing and directing other males under their control and also serving as mediators between the gods and the humans under their dominion. And they ruled militarily, using physical force to preserve the social order, defend the state from its enemies, and maintain their own power. In addition to ruling over others, true men also ruled over themselves, exercising control over their emotions and engaging in measured exercise, rest, sexual relations, and diet, lest they get soft and give in to feminine excess.

What of course becomes obvious from this description of the ideal male is that it is restricted to the elite. Accordingly,

> elite males deemed unmanly all those at the bottom of the social hierarchy, as well as those outside of the Roman empire and thus outside of the social hierarchy altogether. Slaves, "barbarians," and conquered nations as a whole were considered nonmen and frequently feminized by elite male authors.[2]

This socially constructed notion of masculinity thus provides one more resource the elite utilized to legitimate their social power and normalize the status quo. For real men must naturally control and be in control. That is simply the natural order of things and reflective of the divine will that created men. In other words, this notion of manliness provides a philosophical and religious underpinning for a circular and yet eminently useful truth for the elite: real men rule, and those who rule sexually, paternally, politically, and militarily, with self-control, are the real men.

---

1. Much of the following is dependent on Brittany E. Wilson's *Unmanly Men: Refigurations of Masculinity in Luke–Acts* (Oxford: Oxford University Press, 2015), 39–75.
2. Wilson, *Unmanly Men*, 41–42.

2. FAMILY MATTERS: KINSHIP

From well before the earliest Old Testament tradition and well beyond the latest New Testament text, kinship was a fundamental social unit throughout the Mediterranean world. For most during this span of time, kinship played a critical role in determining one's identity, religious commitments, social and economic status, and even one's spouse.

The importance of kinship goes hand in hand with the reality that nearly all in the biblical era tended toward a "collectivist personality." In contrast to the individualism of modern North Americans and Europeans, the self-awareness of Israelites, early Christians, and the others sharing their world was inseparable from the groups of which they were members. The group defined the self and the self was only intelligible as part of the group. "The collectivist personality is thus a person whose total self-awareness emphatically depends on such group embeddedness," writes Bruce Malina.[3] Kinship, family relations, was the primary unit of identity in the ancient Mediterranean. It was that which was most important to know about one's self and others: "To whom do you and I belong?" It all started at home.

One's family unit defined one's occupation, social location, and honor. Males generally followed in the trade of their fathers, which also likely determined their economic opportunity and access to resources. Those resources were to be shared by family members but distributed according to patriarchal rank and birth order within the family unit. The act of naming, especially in the case of male heirs, reflected family pedigree and was the means by which a child (biological or adopted) was claimed by parents and grafted into the household. For those sons who survived into adulthood, the name served as a basic marker of identity, honor, access to resources, and familial rights. Along with those rights came responsibilities, such as contributing to the productivity of the home, caring for elderly parents, and safeguarding and promoting family honor. Male offspring were also charged with the task of continuing the family name by producing, or in some cases adopting, male heirs.

The combination of patriarchy and kinship entailed that the life of a female always revolved around a male provider and, when fortunate, birthing male heirs. Women, with very few exceptions, simply did not have access to social location, honor, or resources apart from a father, uncle, brother, son, or other family member that could provide her with a place in his household. The same is true for children, male and female.

3. Bruce Malina, *The New Testament World: Insights from Cultural Anthropology*, 3rd ed. (Louisville: Westminster John Knox, 2001), 63.

It is for this reason that the fate of widows and orphans—note here that in antiquity one was considered an orphan if he or she did not have a *father*—was especially precarious if they remained unconnected to a male family member. Prostitution, destitution, or slavery claimed many widows and orphans unclaimed by male kin. Many of these unfortunate persons became nobodies in the fullest possible sense.

In contrast to our nuclear family consisting of two generations, family units in antiquity were households often including three or even four generations, with extended family often living in close proximity to one another. Males would continue living in their family households or in a separate dwelling nearby, while women would move to their husbands' families. It was common, however, for marriages to be arranged between extended kin as closely related as first cousins.

Family was the basic unit of sustenance, identity, and honor. But we must also understand that kinship was a mode of belonging that could transcend biological connection. What I have been describing so far in relation to kinship and family structure is the norm within the ancient Mediterranean region. However, in this ancient world there were all sorts of cataclysmic threats to the stability and sustenance of family: disease, famine, war, socioeconomic oppression, indebtedness, and slavery, among others. It was not uncommon for otherwise stable family units to be disrupted and even destroyed, and for many individuals born into slavery to lack anything resembling a biological household. But this did not necessarily mean that such individuals were permanently bereft of any sort of collective association. *Fictive kinship* is a term used by cultural anthropologists to describe the reality that there were multiple forms of family-like associations in the ancient world. Fictive, or "pseudo," kinship often took the form of groups of clients constituted by their commitment to a common patron. Such groupings were governed by the roles, obligations, and responsibilities between the patron and his or her clients, and by the clients' mutual calling to remain loyal to the patron and to some extent one another. For instance, slaves were often considered part of the households they served, and thus granted rights and responsibilities as members of that household, though the benefits they received corresponded to their rank within that family unit. As noted above, individuals could be adopted into a household. Rarer, but not uncommon in the New Testament era, are voluntary associations, such as groups forming around a common trade or even a teacher, that draw on elements of kinship to structure themselves, to establish a sense of group identity and honor, and to clarify expectations and responsibilities.

It was also common to apply kinship language and concepts to much larger social groups that also define one's sense of identity, such as the sense that Israel is united by a single ancestor (Father Abraham), whose bloodline needed to remain pure in order to maintain the integrity and honor of this family (thus circumcision and prohibitions against marrying outside of Israel). Another example of *remote kinship* that overlaps with politics is the tendency for the elite to stylize the state as a family unit, with the head patron (king, emperor) as "father" presiding over an extended household arranged in hierarchical order. (Note that even a society as far removed from the ancient world as modern-day America is not immune from a sense of remote kinship: those residing in the White House are commonly labeled the "first family," which suggests some sense of collective identity among Americans.) Similarly, polytheistic traditions also portrayed the divine pantheon as a family unit, with exceptional earthly rulers sometimes joining its ranks as adopted sons (e.g., Pharaohs, Greek and Roman rulers, even the king of Israel [see Ps 2:7; Isa 9:6–7]), and the rest serving as slaves in the households of the gods. In short, there were multiple layers of kinship in the ancient world, and each layer had the potential to shape one's sense of collective personality and identity in varying degrees.

3. THE COOL KID WINS, UNTIL HE LOSES: HONOR AND SHAME

Kinship was an elemental institution in the biblical world: it governed personal identity, religious commitment, sexual activity, marriage, vocation, social location, and access to resources. Another fundamental, and overlapping, institution shaping life in the ancient world commonly identified by cultural anthropologists was that of politics. On a broader scale, this institution governed and legitimated the social location of its members, the distribution of resources, the worship of particular deities, and the use of persuasive and physical force to attain collective goals.

Here I want to focus in on one dimension of the broad institution of politics, the maintenance and achievement of social location. As discussed above, the Greco-Roman world was steeply stratified, with social location being determined in large measure by one's kinship group and its proximity to those in power. It was also common for elite families to become intertwined via marriage, thus further establishing the mutual, elevated status of both groups as now connected kin. Yet, a critical dimension of social life that could impact social location within peer groups, and even elevate or reduce one's social location, were the pivotal values of honor and shame.[4]

Much of ancient society revolved around the increase and loss of honor. Put simply and helpfully by Bruce Malina,

> Honor is the value of a person in his or her own eyes (that is, one's claim to worth) *plus* that person's value in the eyes of his or her social group. Honor is a claim to worth along with the social acknowledgement of worth.[5]

Relatedly, shame—in a positive sense—refers to one's *sense* of shame, one's sensitivity to one's own reputation, the opinion of others, and the honor rating of others. This is the kind of shame we still refer to today when someone scolds, "Have you no shame?!" A person with shame in this sense is one who accepts or respects norms for human interaction and recognizes social boundaries. So, in this instance, shame is a good thing. But negative shame is not. Cultural anthropologists use the same word as a verb to refer to the act of being shamed. This occurs when one aspires to increase their social status—when one seeks honor—and that quest for honor is not socially validated. So, if I were to show up at a faculty meeting wearing bell-bottom jeans, a silk muscle shirt, and a plaid sport coat, and exclaim to my peers, "Gee whiz, I am really groovy!" and they (understandably) were to respond, "Well, actually Professor Kuhn, you are really *not*," then I would have been shamed. Shaming also occurs when someone or some family member acts in ways that violate social norms. So, for instance (and this is strictly hypothetical), if a son were to play video games on his phone during a church service while grunting and gesticulating signs of success or failure, he would bring shame to the rest of his family. I know this use of terminology is rather counterintuitive, but when you act shamelessly (or badly) in the ancient world, you (and your kinship group) get shamed by others.

Now honor could be either *ascribed* or *acquired.* "Ascribed honor" is honor claimed by and granted to a person due to their kinship group or their association with high-status persons and groups outside of their kinship group. For instance, if you were born into a prestigious and powerful family, you would likely be granted honor due to your membership in that family. Or, let's say all of the pieces of your early life fell fortuitously in place and you found yourself a member of the emperor's court at a young age. You would also be ascribed honor due to your membership in that elite group. Let's imagine again that your astute ser-

---

4. For a helpful and often-cited discussion of the values of honor and shame, see Malina, *New Testament World*, 27–57. The following summary of honor is indebted to Malina's discussion.

5. Malina, *New Testament World*, 30.

vice caught the emperor's eye, and you were appointed as one of the emperor's trusted advisors. Here again you would gain honor not only by your gifted service but also by virtue of your association to another. The emperor's public recognition of you as a chief advisor would ascribe you honor in the eyes of the rest of the court and his loyal subjects (even if they were very jealous of you).

"Acquired honor" is honor that you gain by excelling over others. In other words, this is honor granted to you not simply because of your association with others but by demonstrating your mastery in the eyes of others. How could such mastery be displayed? Undoubtedly, there were many activities that could potentially enhance a person's reputation: acts of heroism, the donation of funds to a public project, a distinguished military career or other service (as in the example above), eloquent oration, control of one's children, among others. Beyond these, a common form of social exchange often termed *challenge and response* also played a pivotal role in the gain and loss of honor. Challenge and response "is sort of a constant social tug of war, a game of social push and shove."[6] It typically contained the following elements and structure:

> Challenge-response within the context of honor is a sort of interaction in at least three phases: (1) the challenge in terms of some action (word, deed, or both) on the part of the challenger; (2) the perception of the message by both the individual to whom it is directed and the public at large; and (3) the reaction of the receiving individual and the evaluation of the reaction on the part of the public.[7]

Malina and others assume that this form of social exchange was exceedingly common, that it characterized, in fact, nearly all of one's interaction with those outside of one's kinship group.[8] I suspect that some social interaction occurred that wasn't so conflicted, but the gospels and other writings reveal that challenge-response was indeed a frequent form of interaction in Mediterranean culture. People were hungry for honor, and they often sought to outdo one another in obtaining it, or to limit the amount of honor held by a perceived rival. In short, Greco-Roman society, especially among the elite and others wanting to achieve a higher social level, was highly competitive. Social jockeying to gain closer proximity to cherished patrons, generous benefaction in the form of monuments or public structures, challenge-and-riposte exchanges,

6. Malina, *New Testament World*, 33.

7. Malina, *New Testament World*, 33. To readers of the canonical gospels, this form of social exchange will likely strike them as familiar. We will discuss Luke's use of the *chreia* or pronouncement story form in chapter 5.

8. Malina, *New Testament World*, 36.

the amassing and display of wealth—all such activities took place within an agonistic context in which the goal was to outdo one another in the acquisition of honor, and thus achieve the position and power to which honor provided access.

4. ELITE AND ELITIST

This agonistic pursuit of honor presumed and manifested a worldview in which all humans were not equal. Most among the elite would have held an account of themselves and their kin that sharply distinguished them from the rest of the population. By virtue of their birth, kinship group (actual or "fictive"), and place in society, by virtue of their ascribed and acquired honor, the elite saw themselves and their fellow elite as superior members of humanity. They embraced a worldview in which their pedigree, elevated sense of morality, and divine mandate included them as among a select few whose worth and potential for good was greater than those outside of that group.[9] These perceptions of elevated worth—and the divine favor they believed accompanied it—legitimated their near-exclusive access to and control of power and wealth. In other words, the elite made the laws, and rightly so, for they were the educated and virtuous. They established economic policy, for they knew how to best manage resources for the good of the empire and to honor the divine patrons of Rome. They spoke for the gods and goddesses, for they had the training and purity to access the divine mysteries and be the faithful guardians of sacred tradition. They ruled the empire, for their station was sanctioned by the emperor who, in turn, was sanctioned by heaven and was himself either a member of, or closely connected to, the divine realm.

In Jesus's day, the Israelite elite consisted primarily of the Sadducees and Herodians. Deriving their status through pedigree, they belonged to the right families, and thus enjoyed the power, property, and honor due to persons of their status. Their positions were legitimated by their sacred traditions, for the Sadducees, the Israelite Scriptures, and for the Herodians, primarily Roman law (and perhaps, marginally, Israelite tra-

9. Neil Elliott, *The Arrogance of the Nations: Reading Romans in the Shadow of Empire*, Paul in Critical Contexts (Minneapolis: Fortress Press, 2008), 30–33, helpfully lists several examples of what he terms "the hidden transcript of the powerful," in which members of the ruling class express their contempt for and sense of superiority over the lower classes, and the need for brutal rule over them. See also Gildas Hamel, "Poverty and Charity," in *The Oxford Handbook of Jewish Daily Life in Roman Palestine*, ed. Catherine Hezer (Oxford: Oxford University Press, 2010), 316, and David A. Fiensy, *The Social History of Palestine in the Herodian Period: The Land Is Mine*, Studies in the Bible and Early Christianity 20 (Lewiston, NY: Edwin Mellen, 1991), 169–70.

dition). Centered in Jerusalem and overseeing the temple, Sadducees and their scribes were the bearers of their culture's "Great Tradition," believing themselves, and believed by many others, to be those authorized by God to preserve, propound, and practice the teaching and ritual established by the God of Abraham. They were purported to embody the ideal of Israelite faith and practice, and they resourced the Great Tradition through two key political functions: enacting taxes for the temple, the city, and the city's elite, and, along with their lawyers and scribes, enforcing the Tradition through a police force and a court system overseen by the Sanhedrin.[10] Malina and others consider the Pharisees to be non-elites who sought to mediate the Great Tradition, especially its version of the purity codes, to the rural areas beyond the power centers of Palestinian cities (more on this in chapter 5).[11] They were "teachers of Torah," who sought to "correct" the misguided practice of the faith, the "Little Tradition," embraced in villages. They likely faced the challenge of trying to instruct folk for whom consistent attention to the purity and Sabbath regulations as defined by the Pharisees was simply not practical, or even possible. As noted already, the gospels give us the impression that some (but not all) Pharisees embraced the values of the Jerusalem elite. They might not share in their pedigree and the power, but they too are seekers of wealth and honor and resort to shaming others as a means of elevating their own social standing. Further affirmation of their elite mentality is provided by Rabbinic traditions of the first and second centuries CE, which consider wealth a sign of God's blessing, and poverty a sign of God's wrath.[12]

5. GODLY MEN

Roman religion presumed a cosmic order that paralleled the socioeconomic stratification and patterns of Roman society. The gods, themselves arranged in a loose hierarchy, were the patrons of the empire: to them was due honor in order to ensure their blessing upon the Roman people. Accordingly, allotments from the resources of the empire were to be placed at their feet in the forms of tithes, sacrifices, and offerings. The belief in divine patronage and the dutiful practice of making offerings to the gods by the Roman people (and most others) not only paralleled but normalized and implicitly justified the similar ordering of the

---

10. Malina, *New Testament World*, 87.

11. Malina, *New Testament World*, 88.

12. Dieter Heinrich Reinstorf, "The Rich, the Poor, and the Law," *HTS* 60, no. 1/2 (2004): 345–46.

Roman society and its economy. Just as the divine patrons deserve and require the honor and offerings of the Roman state, so do the earthly patrons of Rome who rule as representatives of the gods.

That the elite who ascended to prominent offices served as representatives of the divine is reflected in several features of their appointment. The installation and ongoing celebration of those rulers took place in religious contexts, and prayers were regularly offered on their behalf. Moreover, by virtue of their office, nearly all public officials served in a cultic capacity as religious authorities.

> All those who held authority in public life, at whatever level, magistrate, promagistrate, legate, centurion, college president, or president of a local district, and so on—were also responsible for the cult of the community that they led. . . . Every important decision involving religion, every innovation and disagreement relating to a religious problem that affected the public cult or other cults that were celebrated in public, fell within their domain.[13]

An important dimension, therefore, of the honor due to civic leaders was their role as cultic and religious leaders, and their mediation of the nexus between human and divine spheres of reality. To put it rather baldly, the elite "used their wealth and influence to benefit the city in exchange for the social prestige and authority that their offices conferred upon them, including the implicit right to regulate the city's relations with its gods."[14] In short, the elites' role as mediators of the divine was contingent upon their social location and economic patronage. And their representative function as religious authorities, on whom the gods' favor rested, in turn legitimated their control of those positions *and* the means by which they achieved them.

The Roman tendency to associate political power with a divine mandate to rule is also manifested in what is often called the "imperial cult." The imperial cult is probably best described as a loosely connected and varied set of practices and perspectives that associate the emperor and even the imperial family with the divine realm.[15] With the elevation of the emperor as the sole head of the Roman Empire, to whom all political and economic allegiance was due, there also developed the tendency to regard him as a transcendent, divine-like figure. Since no other person held greater powers or honors than those of Augustus, "the emperor and

---

13. John Scheid, *An Introduction to Roman Religion*, trans. Janet Lloyd (Bloomington: Indiana University Press, 2003), 129.

14. James B. Rives, *Religion in the Roman Empire*, Blackwell Ancient Religions 2 (Oxford: Blackwell, 2007), 115.

15. Much of the present paragraph borrows from the helpful discussion of the imperial cult in Rives, *Religion in the Roman Empire*, 148–57.

his family were granted honors equal to those enjoyed by the gods" by elite and peasant alike.[16] Such exaltation was manifested in various ways. Octavian initiated the practice of deifying deceased emperors by promoting the cult of the "Deified Julius," constructing a temple to honor the new god and appointing a priest as custodian. With Augustus's own death a formal procedure for deification of deceased emperors began to take shape, and temples to honor deceased emperors started springing up throughout the empire. Most Romans did not worship the emperors while living, but many did worship the current emperor's *numen* (divine power) or *genius* (guardian spirit) in temples dedicated to those entities, a practice that Octavian himself no doubt encouraged by taking on the title "Augustus" ("majestic," "venerable"). However, there were some provincial cults that worshipped living emperors as gods, and the emperors Caligula and Domitian demanded that they be treated as gods while alive, while others such as Claudius more ambiguously portrayed themselves on coinage in the guise of specific deities. Sacrifices were regularly offered on behalf of living emperors, including in the Jerusalem temple! The Roman cultic calendar celebrated notable accomplishments and events in the lives of the emperors and other members of the imperial family. Despite the various forms and practices of the imperial cult, central to its mission was the notion that the emperor was to be "envisioned as the key point of intersection between the divine and human spheres."[17]

Note the political, social, and economic significance of this religious belief. Roman power, social structure, and economy all derived their focus, form, and meaning from the empire's chief patron, the emperor. And the emperor himself was regarded as "the epiphany of divine power in the hands of a mortal."[18] He was the gods' steward to the Roman people. He himself ruled with the gods' authority and blessing. According to the various manifestations of the imperial cult, that reality was to be celebrated and cherished.

SEEING THESE INSIGHTS IN ACTION

As in the previous chapter, we will now turn to the biblical text to see how some of these insights as enhanced by cultural anthropology might yield important exegetical dividends.

16. Scheid, *Roman Religion*, 164–65.
17. Rives, *Religion in the Roman Empire*, 155.
18. Scheid, *Roman Religion*, 165.

MARK 3:1–6

I have mentioned already that Mark's Gospel draws its recipients into the inevitable collision he unveils between the values of Rome and the values of God's kingdom. Mark does not waste time in ramping up that conflict to a fevered pitch. Already, at the start of chapter 3, we read:

> [1] Again he entered the synagogue, and a man was there who had a withered hand. [2] They watched him to see whether he would cure him on the sabbath, so that they might accuse him. [3] And he said to the man who had the withered hand, "Come forward." [4] Then he said to them, "Is it lawful to do good or to do harm on the sabbath, to save life or to kill?" But they were silent. [5] He looked around at them with anger; he was grieved at their hardness of heart and said to the man, "Stretch out your hand." He stretched it out, and his hand was restored. [6] The Pharisees went out and immediately conspired with the Herodians against him, how to destroy him.

We often treat this conflict as a dispute over "doctrine," of Jesus wrangling with his fellow Israelites over the keeping of Torah. It certainly is that: "They watched him to see whether he would cure him on the sabbath, so that they might accuse him" (v. 2). But the conflict in this scene transcends competing interpretations of the law. This passage is also a dispute about honor, shame, authority, the Great Tradition, and claims over divine mandate. First, note that this scene concludes a series of "controversy dialogues" spanning 2:1–3:6, most of which feature repeated challenge-riposte sequences. Jesus performs an action, he is challenged by religious authorities, and he responds.

	Action	Challenge	Response
1–12	Jesus heals and pronounces forgiveness	Scribes: "It is blasphemy."	"Which is easier to say ...?"
13–17	Jesus calls Levi	Pharisees: "Why does he eat with tax collectors and sinners?"	"I have come to call not the righteous but sinners."
23–28	Disciples plucking grain	Pharisees: "This is not lawful."	"The sabbath was made for humankind ..."

Knowing that challenge-riposte sequences were a common form of social exchange used to negotiate claims of honor and authority is one more indicator of the conflicted character of these scenes. Perhaps this is already quite apparent, but this insight further affirms the dark and tense mood of these passages. Even more importantly, against their social backdrop these sequences lead us to recognize that the primary issue coming to the fore is not simply what it means to follow Torah but who has the wisdom and authority to discern God's will and mediate God's mercy. The Pharisees, scribes, and others aligned with the Israelite elite refuse to recognize the presence and power of God's kingdom in Jesus, despite the miraculous healings he has performed. Thus, they challenge him at every turn in the attempt to shame and discredit him. From the perspective of the Pharisees and other Israelite leaders, it is bad enough that Jesus is undermining the correct understanding of God's instruction. But perhaps even more threatening, and even more blasphemous in their view, he is challenging their hold on the Great Tradition, and perhaps the Great Tradition itself, which restricted access to God's mercy through the mediation of the temple elite. Now—through Jesus's ministry—healing and even forgiveness (see Mark 2:1–12) are given to the marginalized apart from proper ritual, remuneration, or sacred space! Jesus continues the bestowal of God's blessing and forgiveness John began *outside of* Jerusalem (1:4–5). By claiming the authority to interpret Torah and mediate God's mercy, by claiming to be sent by God to enact a divine mandate (see 1:14–15, 37–38; 2:10, 18–22, 28), Jesus was threatening the carefully circumscribed matrices of political, economic, social, and religious power cultivated by the elite and their retainers. In sum, the conflict unfolding in this scene and the ones surrounding it is about much more than how one should behave on the Sabbath. It is really about who has the right to teach God's will and steward God's grace.

The chilling notice of 3:6 provides further indication of the grave issues at hand and the elites' view of Jesus as an intolerable deviant. Pharisees and Herodians are not likely allies. But they are both deeply staked in the status quo, and so they readily join forces to counter the threat before them. Their response is immediate and extreme. There is no room for negotiation, no cautious waiting to see how things unfold. Jesus must be destroyed.

LUKE 1:57–66

Our brief encounter with Mark 3:1–6 helped us to see how cultural anthropology's insights on honor, shame, and elite claims to a divine mandate deepen our engagement and understanding of this text. We now turn to Luke's infancy narrative to illustrate how knowledge of the centrality of kinship in ancient Mediterranean society can also be useful.

John—the son of Elizabeth and recently muted Zechariah—is born! Here is the advent of one who will "make ready a people prepared for the Lord" (see 1:13–18). However, John's birth sparks a controversy that becomes the focus of the account: What shall this child be named? Accordingly, it stands to reason that the importance and practice of kinship in the first century is a critical component of this passage. Keeping this in mind might enable us to solve a vexing interpretive issue that has long plagued interpreters of this story, while also helping us to appreciate more fully the poignant character of the tale. Due to the complexity of this story, it will take a bit more space for us to unpack.

[57] Now the time came for Elizabeth to give birth, and she bore a son. [58] Her neighbors and relatives heard that the Lord had shown his great mercy to her, and they rejoiced with her.
[59] On the eighth day they came to circumcise the child, and they were going to name him Zechariah after his father. [60] But his mother said, "No; he is to be called John." [61] They said to her, "None of your relatives has this name." [62] Then they began motioning to his father to find out what name he wanted to give him. [63] He asked for a writing-tablet and wrote, "His name is John." And all of them were amazed. [64] Immediately his mouth was opened and his tongue freed, and he began to speak, praising God. [65] Fear came over all their neighbors, and all these things were talked about throughout the entire hill country of Judea. [66] All who heard them pondered them and said, "What then will this child become?" For, indeed, the hand of the Lord was with him.

One of the key interpretive challenges elicited by this engaging tale is how to understand the amazement of the crowds in response to Zechariah's affirmation of the name spoken by Elizabeth (v. 63b). Nearly all commentators agree that the crowd's amazement is cast by Luke as a response to what they perceive as God's miraculous intervention.[19]

---

19. Although *thuamazo* can express amazement at an occurrence not linked to a divinely ordained event (such as in Luke 1:21; 7:9; and 11:38), in the overwhelming majority of instances in which it is used in Luke–Acts it is a response to events or revelation attributed either to God (2:18; 2:33; 24:12; Acts 2:7; 7:31; 13:41), Jesus (4:22; 8:25; 9:43; 11:14; 20:26; 24:4; Acts 3:12), or to the manifestation of God's power in Jesus's disciples (Acts 3:12; 4:13).

Luke's concluding summary to this scene confirms his intent to portray the events surrounding John's birth—"all these things"—as manifestations of God's intervention (vv. 65–66): "For indeed, the hand of the Lord was with him."

What is far less clear, however, is how Zechariah's naming of the child constitutes a manifestation of divine action that leads to the amazement of the crowd. Because Luke tells us that the crowd "began motioning to his father to find out what name he wanted to give him" (v. 62), many conclude that Zechariah was not only rendered mute by Gabriel's punitive sign but deaf as well. Accordingly, they propose that the crowd marvels at Zechariah's response because—since he could not have heard Elizabeth's insistence that the child be named John—his giving of the same name would have been such an extraordinary coincidence that it could only be attributed to God's miraculous intervention.[20]

In my view, however, this proposal fails for two main reasons. First, it seems to me unlikely that if Luke intends us to see Zechariah as both mute and deaf he would have waited until this point in the narrative to indicate this to the reader and would have chosen to do so in such an indirect fashion. What Luke has instead repeatedly and singularly identified as the consequence of Gabriel's punitive sign is Zechariah's inability to speak (vv. 20–22) including here in verse 63 (writing tablet) and verse 64 (tongue loosed). Consequently, a more plausible explanation is that Luke intends us to view the crowd's motioning to Zechariah not as an attempt to communicate in rudimentary sign language because Zechariah is deaf, but simply their attempt to get his attention so that they may inquire of him concerning the child's name. This is consistent with the meaning and use of *enneuo*, which basically means to gesture or signal with the hands.[21] Narratively, it functions to bring Zechariah in from the periphery of the account and now place him at its center.

Second, the proposal fails to account for the arrangement and focus of the pericope itself, *and* dimensions of its cultural context that are crucial to making sense of it. Luke shapes his account to emphasize the countercultural and sacrificial, not the coincidental, character of Elizabeth and Zechariah's announcement of a name for their son. The amazement of the crowd, like the passage itself, is centered squarely on the

---

20. E.g., Raymond E. Brown, *The Birth of the Messiah: A Commentary on the Infancy Narratives in the Gospels of Matthew and Luke*, rev. ed. (New York: Doubleday, 1993), 369; Joseph A. Fitzmyer, *The Gospel According to Luke I–IX*, AB 28 (New York: Doubleday, 1981), 381; John Nolland, *Luke 1–9:20*, WBC 35a (Waco, TX: Word, 1989), 33, 79; Joel B. Green, *The Gospel of Luke*, NICNT (Grand Rapids: Eerdmans, 1997), 109; François Bovon, *Luke 1: A Commentary on the Gospel of Luke 1:1–9:50*, Hermeneia (Minneapolis: Fortress Press, 2002), 71.

21. BAGD, 267.

cultural oddity of John's naming. Take note of the structure and pac-
ing of the birth and circumcision accounts. The moment of John's birth,
while important to Luke, is not where he wants his readers' attention
to linger. This he crisply relays in perfunctory fashion: "Now the time
came for Elizabeth to give birth, and she bore a son" (v. 57). An equally
brief account of the ensuing celebration follows, reminding us of the
tremendous blessing God has bestowed upon Elizabeth and Israel, and
the response befitting the manifestation of God's saving work among
them (v. 58). In short, Luke quickly ushers his readers through the birth
of John and on to the day of his circumcision. Here, the pace of the narrative slows considerably as the evangelist invites his readers to ponder
the controversy over the naming of the newborn child (vv. 59–66) and
Zechariah's belated praise celebrating John as the one who goes before
the Lord (vv. 67–80). Hence, the passage as a whole (vv. 57–80) revolves
around these three interlaced concerns: Zechariah's return to faith, what
the child is to be named, and the nature of John's mission.

As Luke shapes the account to center his readers' attentions on these
three foci, he also amplifies the controversial nature of John's naming
through the exchange that takes place between Elizabeth and the well-
wishers. A crowd of neighbors and relatives gather for John's circumcision, and they come ready with a name for the child: "On the eighth
day they came to circumcise the child, and they were going to name
him Zechariah after his father" (v. 59). Elizabeth, however, sternly rejects
the crowd's presumption that the child would be named after the father
(v. 60). Unfortunately, the NRSV fails to capture the force of Elizabeth's
dismissal. The Greek, *ouchi*, is an adverbial form of the negation *ou*
("not"), likely emphatic when followed by *alla*, and used in response to
a question when an affirmative answer is expected (see also Luke 12:51).
Thus it is better rendered "Not so!"[22] The emphatic nature of Elizabeth's
response, coupled with the crowd's ensuing retort, draw out the conflicted character of the scene. Equally important, they also focus attention on the transgression of social custom as the point of dispute in the
naming of the child: "None of your relatives has this name" (v. 61). In
sum, the plotting and conflicted character of the passage point to the
countercultural oddity of the naming as the focus of the people's amazement when the name is affirmed by Zechariah, not the supposedly coincidental manner in which it is bestowed.

Of course, more is at stake than simply a name, as the convergence of
important literary and cultural trends in this passage also helps us to see.

22. Harold K. Moulton, ed., *The Analytical Greek Lexicon Revised* (Grand Rapids: Eerdmans, 1977), 294.

Similar to annunciations, birth accounts in historical and biographical works of the time often served to express the essential qualities and significance of the child who was born, as is clear from both Greco-Roman and Old Testament precedents recounting the births of key figures.[23] The pairing of John's birth and circumcision with Zechariah's canticle further elaborating the import of his son (vv. 67–80), as well as the clear connections between the birth account and the annunciation of John's birth (compare 1:67–80 with 1:13–17), confirm that the birth story is also meant to fulfill the role of disclosing fundamental features of John's person and purpose. Moreover, as we discussed earlier, kinship was the most basic category of one's identity in antiquity, determining (almost always) one's social unit, status, and vocation. The act of naming—in the broader Greco-Roman world and also within Israel—was the fundamental means by which a child was claimed by parents and grafted into a household. For those children who survived into adulthood, one's name served a basic marker of one's personal identity, social location, honor, access to resources, and familial rights. Along with the rights established by one's name came responsibilities, such as contributing to the productivity of the home, caring for elderly parents, and upholding the family's honor. Male offspring were also charged with the task of continuing the family name by producing, or in some cases adopting and renaming, male heirs.

Together, the conventional character of birth accounts and the cultural norms governing kinship and naming lead us to recognize that the essential issue at hand in the naming of John is *who shall define the identity and mission of this child?* The reader knows—it is God. Elizabeth and Zechariah know this as well: he is to be named "John" as Gabriel commanded. The crowd, however, does not know John's true identity and mission, at least not before the loosing of Zechariah's tongue and his song to follow, and so they insist on a name that reflects his parentage or at least his kin.

Noting how these literary and cultural trends amplify the controversy surrounding John's naming and enrich its significance further affirms that the crowd's amazement is directed at Elizabeth and Zechariah's eschewal of social convention in the naming of their son, rather than the not-so-astounding coincidence that parents awaiting the birth of a child would agree on a name. In essence, what Elizabeth and Zechariah are doing is granting their newborn son an identity that is not to be

23. Old Testament parallels include the birth accounts of Jacob, Esau, Moses, and Samuel. Joseph B. Tyson, "The Birth Narratives and the Beginning of Luke's Gospel," *Semeia* 52 (1990): 103, lists biographies of Plato, Alexander the Great, and Apollonius of Tyana as examples of Greco-Roman parallels.

seen primarily in terms of his parentage or kin. They are disassociating John from themselves and honoring the revelation that his significance transcends the blessing his birth has brought to them. Within their cultural context, and especially in light of their particular circumstances, this act of naming is extraordinary. It is no wonder that when Elizabeth announces an appellation outside their kin group, those gathered protest. When Zechariah affirms the selection of the name, it is no wonder that they regard this highly irregular act as another remarkable event surrounding his birth. Then the restoration of Zechariah's faith and voice affirms for the crowd what the controversial name has already suggested: the divinely ordained significance of this child. Appropriately, they ponder, "What then will this child become?" as they reflect on the full chain of events accompanying his birth and circumcision (v. 66). As if in answer, Zechariah's hymn then commences (vv. 67–80), providing additional details on the identity and mission of John.

In concert with other important factors, such as the parallels Luke weaves in this account to other biblical characters, and the parallelism he draws between Jesus and John throughout this infancy narrative, these literary and cultural cues help us appreciate the focus of the crowd's response.[24] Yet they also help us discern that Luke was aiming for readers to appreciate an additional dimension of the scene that may transcend the immediate perception of the well-wishers. Luke crafts the passage, pointing his audience to the countercultural oddity John's name represents. In doing so, he not only draws readers' attention to Elizabeth and Zechariah's faithfulness, and John's unique mission as the one who will go before the Lord God, but also to the *sacrifice* this act of naming represents. The elderly, barren couple, whose unceasing prayer for a child was miraculously answered, identify their beloved son, source of great joy, rejoicing, and vindication, not in relationship to themselves or their family, as would be expected, but in relationship to God's purpose and plan. The crowd's protest and amazement help readers appreciate what is at stake. "What do you mean he's not to be named Zechariah? What? John?! Who the heck is John? Where's Zechariah? He'll set his wife straight!" But like Hannah and Elkanah, Elizabeth and Zechariah accept God's will that their beloved son is called to a mission that will ultimately take him beyond their household, and from them. When Samuel was weaned, Hannah gathered up the child for whom she had desperately yearned and traveled back to Shiloh. "She left him there for the Lord"

---

24. For a fuller discussion of the passage, see Karl Kuhn, "Deaf or Defiant: The Literary, Cultural, and Affective-Rhetorical Keys to the Naming of John (Luke 1:57–80)," *CBQ* 75 (2013): 486–503.

(1 Sam 1:28). Here, Zechariah and Elizabeth do the same. Their naming of John was not a mindless recitation of Gabriel's command. The defiant tone of Elizabeth's "Not so!" and Zechariah's scrawl tell us that they realized well what was at stake. And yet readers who have sympathized with Elizabeth and Zechariah and rejoiced in their blessing of a son are now led to recognize and participate in the sense of loss that also pervades this scene, to hear the sorrow mixed in with Elizabeth and Zechariah's righteous resolve. Luke reveals through this affectively laden moment that the restoration of Israel will be accompanied by personal sacrifice. This is the first of several indications throughout the infancy narrative that the coming of God's kingdom will come at a cost, not only for the proud and Israel's enemies, but for the faithful as well (see also 2:34–35). Zechariah and Elizabeth prove up to the challenge, even if it means that they have to leave their beloved son, John, for the Lord.

4.

Biblical Writings as Texts of Resistance and Conformity

In the opening chapter, I overviewed three paradigms that represent some of the different ways anthropologists understand the shape and function of human cultures. The *structural-functionalist* model presupposes that every society is a relatively stable and well-integrated system. Nearly every element in that society exists for the purpose of maintaining the status quo. Thus, its various subsystems—or institutions—such as family, government, economics, education, and religion operate harmoniously within that society with common values and norms. The natural trend, in this view, is toward stability and cooperation, and change is seen as deviation.

In contrast, the *conflict theory* model views societies as composed of various social groups with competing interests and agendas. Each of these groups utilizes coercive tactics to protect the distinctive interests of its own members. Though at times groups will cooperate with others when it suits their own agendas, constraint and conflict are the norm rather than cooperation and harmony. As a result, according to this view, social structures and institutions trend toward instability and change.

Holding a middle ground of sorts between these two macro-models is a third, the *symbolic model*. This model presupposes that individual and group behavior is organized around the symbolic meanings and expectations attached to objects that are socially valued, such as the self, others, nature, time, space, and the sacred. The patterns of behavior that characterize interactions between these symbolized agents trend toward both maintaining social equilibrium in ways consistent with shared symbolic meanings, and ongoing readjustment in light of conflicting agendas, competing worldviews, and evolving circumstances. In this view, social structures facilitate differentiation and cooperation, constraint and facilitation.

I tend to gravitate toward the symbolic model in my understanding of human societies, and a dialectal pattern between conformity and conflict with respect to human relations as people negotiate their somewhat shared and somewhat competing agendas and worldviews. In my mind, this "middle view" best captures both the presence of conflict and cooperation within human societies and the reality that most people have a sense of identity and purpose that gives symbolic meaning to their alliances, enmities, and behavior. I review these macro-models here, however, not so much to argue for any one in particular, but to point out that each model, including the structural-functionalist, recognizes the reality of deviation, instability, and change. Even though societies establish powerful and deeply entrenched systems or movements that to some degree facilitate stability, or perpetuate the agendas of certain stakeholders, or cultivate shared understandings of communities, persons, and contexts, resistance is an inevitable corollary. When power is embodied and symbolized in ways that some, even if a small minority, view as illegitimate, "social movements" will arise to resist those practices of power, rhetorically and even materially. "Countermovements," on the other hand, seek to reassert the value and propriety of the social norms that are being challenged by social movements. In the words of McCarthy and Zald, "a *social movement* is a set of opinions and beliefs in a population representing preferences for changing some elements of the social structure and/or reward distribution of a society."[1] Such movements often lead to the formation of "social movement organizations" that identify their goals with the preferences of the social movement to which they are aligned and attempt to implement those goals. A countermovement, then, is "a set of opinions and beliefs in a population opposed to social movement."[2] Malina adds, "Countermovements oppose change. They focus on stability and permanence."[3]

The writings of the Old and New Testaments contain a mix of literature borne out of contexts of social movement and countermovement. Some of these traditions, many in fact, are "resistance literature," written to call the faithful to a belief system and lifestyle in many respects opposed to the power relations and norms that rule their world. Other texts are "conformist literature," writings that resist social movements in order to call their communities back to ways of perceiving and behaving that preserve order, facilitate peaceful coexistence within an oppres-

1. John D. McCarthy and Myer M. Zald, "Resource Mobilization and Social Movements: A Partial Theory," *American Journal of Sociology* 82, no. 6 (1977): 20.
2. McCarthy and Zald, "Resource Mobilization and Social Movements," 20.
3. Bruce Malina, *The New Testament World: Insights from Cultural Anthropology*, 3rd ed. (Louisville: Westminster John Knox, 2001), 213.

sive society, or reclaim what they believe are important elements of their communities' covenantal obligations to God.

In this chapter, we will explore examples of biblical texts of resistance that enact and inspire social movement, and texts of conformity that represent countermovements opposing change agents within the Israelite and early Christian communities. The purpose of the chapter is to illustrate the usefulness of these models of "social movement" and "countermovement" for developing a greater awareness of the social and rhetorical dynamics reflected in many biblical traditions. Relatedly, an additional benefit of these models is that they can help us recognize and better understand occasions in which the biblical authors expressed contrary opinions on the very same matter.

TEXTS OF RESISTANCE

LUKE 2:1–14 AND ACTS 4

Throughout the preceding episodes of the infancy narrative, including (as we saw) in Mary's hymn (1:46–56), Luke stresses that the kingdom inaugurated in the conceptions and births of John and Jesus is one that will turn the tables on the current world order. Luke's infancy narrative, and Luke-Acts as a whole, is resistance literature powerfully and eloquently advocating for the social movement the evangelist is urging Theophilus and others to join. Luke calls Theophilus and others to leave behind the world shaped by Rome, to abandon their allegiance to Caesar as its Sovereign, and instead to embrace God's realm and follow the one who is truly Lord. The crescendo of Luke's portrayal of this "upsidedown" world in the infancy narrative and call for resistance takes place here in the story of Jesus's birth.

[1] In those days a decree went out from Emperor Augustus that all the world should be registered. [2] This was the first registration and was taken while Quirinius was governor of Syria. [3] All went to their own towns to be registered. [4] Joseph also went from the town of Nazareth in Galilee to Judea, to the city of David called Bethlehem, because he was descended from the house and family of David. [5] He went to be registered with Mary, to whom he was engaged and who was expecting a child. [6] While they were there, the time came for her to deliver her child. [7] And she gave birth to her firstborn son and wrapped him in bands of cloth, and laid him in a manger, because there was no place for them in the inn.

[8] In that region there were shepherds living in the fields, keeping watch over their flock by night. [9] Then an angel of the Lord stood before them,

and the glory of the Lord shone around them, and they were terrified. [10] But the angel said to them, "Do not be afraid; for see—I am bringing you good news of great joy for all the people: [11] to you is born this day in the city of David a Savior, who is the Messiah, the Lord. [12] This will be a sign for you: you will find a child wrapped in bands of cloth and lying in a manger." [13] And suddenly there was with the angel a multitude of the heavenly host, praising God and saying,

[14] "Glory to God in the highest heaven,
and on earth peace among those whom he favors!"

Yet as the passage opens, it is the one known throughout the Mediterranean region and beyond as Lord who speaks and moves "all the world" to action (2:1). We begin in the throne room of Rome, as Caesar Augustus, the Roman emperor and father of the empire, orders a census to be taken. Caesar wants to take stock of his subjects and possessions, the objects of his rule and sources of revenue (think taxation). His word is spoken, his underlings such as Quirinius, governor of Syria, make it happen, and the rest of the world has no choice but to comply with this "penetrating symbol of Roman overlordship."[4] And so, "all went to their own towns to be registered" (v. 3). The father of Jesus is no exception: "Joseph also went from the town of Nazareth in Galilee to Judea, to the city of David called Bethlehem" (v. 4). Caesar's command rules the cosmos, or so it seems.

Scholars have long noted and debated a serious problem with Luke's chronology here. As many point out, reliable historical sources place the reign of Quirinius and the census undertaken while he was governor several years later in 6 CE.[5] We will not engage this debate except to note that scholars commonly view the census as a device to get Mary and Joseph to Bethlehem so that Jesus's birthplace fulfills the prophecy found in Micah 5:2–4 (cf. Matt 2:1–6). Luke's interest in Bethlehem for these reasons seems likely, but the census serves other interests as well. If Luke, along with Matthew, understands Jesus's birth in Bethlehem as the divinely ordained fulfillment of Micah's prophecy, then notice how the mighty rule of Caesar is already being undercut in the opening verses of Luke's account. Ironically and unknowingly, Caesar Augustus, the

4. Joel B. Green, *The Gospel of Luke*, NICNT (Grand Rapids: Eerdmans, 1997), 122. For a helpful discussion of how the census would be perceived by most Israelites as a particularly egregious instance of oppressive Roman hegemony, see Richard Horsley, *The Liberation of Christmas: The Infancy Narratives in Social Context* (Eugene, OR: Wipf & Stock, 1989), 33–38.

5. Helpful overviews of the debate can be found in Joseph A. Fitzmyer, *The Gospel According to Luke I–IX*, AB 28 (New York: Doubleday, 1981), 400–405; John Nolland, *Luke 1:1–9:20*, WBC 35a (Waco, TX: Word, 1989), 99–103; and Darrell L. Bock, *Luke 1:1–9:50*, BECNT (Grand Rapids: Baker Academic, 1994), 903–9.

world's venerated sovereign, puts into motion events that lead to the ful-fillment of *God's* will for Israel and all the world. Caesar may rule the cosmos, including Palestine, but Israel's Messiah who will deliver Israel from its enemies is about to be born (cf. 1:71, 74). And Caesar helps bring it all to pass, unknowingly pushing the unborn Jesus to Bethle-hem, that he might be born just as God "spoke through the mouth of his holy prophets from of old" (1:70).

In her song of praise, Mary announced that the coming of her child would result in the bringing down of the powerful from their thrones and the lifting up of the lowly—nothing short of a reversal of the Roman social and economic order (1:52). But even this warning leaves the recip-ient unprepared for Luke's description of Jesus's birth and humble state of his first resting place. In simple, unadorned prose, we are told that Jesus is born, wrapped in bands of cloth, and laid in a feedbox "because there was no place for them in the inn" (2:7). It can't get much lowlier than this. The "inn" (*kataluma*) or hostel-like room adjoining a house is full. None move aside so that the very pregnant and eventually laboring Mary can give birth in the security of even these very meager quarters. So the young couple nestles in among the sheep, goats, and chickens, delivers their child, and employs a manger for a crib. Luke's recipients are con-fronted with an image of Israel's Messiah that could not be more incon-gruous with the pomp and might of Emperor Augustus on his throne, commanding the world at will. The repeated references to the bands of cloth and manger and their function as the "sign" that identifies Jesus (2:7, 12, 16–17) keep these lowly elements in view even as he is exalted by the heavenly host and found by the shepherds.

As the scene shifts from stable to darkened field, we once again encounter a setting far removed from Caesar's seat in Rome: shepherds tending their flocks by night. The lowliness of the shepherds and the locale of the angelic host's appearance to them continue the theme of reversal permeating the passage. Recall our discussion of Roman soci-ety and economy in chapter 2. Shepherds, along with other agricultural workers, were among the large peasant class whose economic servitude fueled the economy of empire and hegemony of Roman rule. More-over, from an Israelite perspective, shepherds would also be in regular contact with contaminating substances and may lack the ability to per-form ablutions (more on this in chapter 5). Yet it is to such as these that the announcement of the kingdom arrives. The reversal inherent in the heavenly host's appearance targets the Israelite elite as well, for "God's glory, normally associated with the temple, is now manifest on a farm!"[6] While Jesus will engage the Israelite elite on their own turf, the manifestation of God's reign will not be confined to their domain or controlled by their patronage. Something radically new is taking place. Luke's account indicates that divine revelation and divine authorization will transcend elite brokerage.

To be sure, the claim that the birth of this Israelite peasant infant, and his manifestation in this agrarian setting so far removed from the center of elite power, poses any sort of meaningful challenge to their rule would by nearly all sane accounts of the time be simply laughable. But this is just the announcement that explodes from the heavenly messengers into the night. Luke crafts the angelic proclamation to amplify (in tandem with 1:26–38) Jesus's divine identity while at the same time composing an implied, but quite apparent, repudiation of Caesar's reign. Luke shapes the angels' testimony so that many of the things celebrated about Caesar and his birth by those allied with Rome are now attributed to this infant lying in a feedbox, whose identity as "Savior, Messiah Lord" reflects the character and identity of Yahweh. In their decision to honor Augustus by beginning the new year on his birthday, the Roman provincial assembly announced,

> Whereas the providence which divinely ordered our lives created with zeal and munificence the most perfect good for our lives by producing Augustus ... for the *benefaction of mankind*, sending us a *savior* who put an end to war ... and whereas the *birthday* of the god marked *for the world* the beginning of *good tidings* through his coming.[7]

The parallels to the angel's announcement in 2:10–11 are apparent:

> Do not be afraid; for see—I am bringing you *good news* of great joy for *all the people*: to you is *born this day* in the city of David a *Savior*, who is the Messiah Lord (my translation).

As Horsley comments, "any reader or hearer of this story in the Hellenistic-Roman world, particularly in Palestine, would have understood here a direct opposition between Caesar, the savior who had supposedly brought peace, and the child proclaimed as the savior, whose birth means peace."[8]

Beyond the Roman celebration of Augustus, there were other claims to Roman lordship that would have been scorched upon the hearts of

---

6. Green, *Luke*, 131.

7. Translation from S. R. F. Price, *Rituals and Power: The Roman Imperial Cult in Asia Minor* (Cambridge: Cambridge University Press, 1984), 54.

8. Horsley, *Liberation of Christmas*, 32–33.

those sympathetic to traditional Israelite hopes. In the aftermath of the Judean revolt in 67–70 CE, Roman supporters added insult to tragedy by claiming that Vespasian, or his son, Titus—the Roman heroes in the defeat of Jerusalem who were later crowned emperors—were the ones who fulfilled the Israelite messianic prophecies of old! The Israelite general turned historian, Josephus, who entered into the service of Titus after the revolt, proclaimed,

> But what more than all else incited them [the Jews] to war was an ambiguous oracle, likewise found in their sacred scriptures, to the effect that at that time one from their own country would become ruler of the world. This they understood to mean someone from their own race, and many of their wise men went astray in their interpretation of it. The oracle, however, in reality signified the sovereignty of Vespasian, who was proclaimed Emperor on Jewish soil.[9]

In not-so-subtle contrast to the prevailing Roman propaganda of the day, Luke's challenge dramatically relayed is this: the Israelite infant lying in a feedbox among sheep, goats, cattle, and fowl, undermines the significance of Caesar and Rome, because in his humility and lowliness this one named "Savior" and "Messiah Lord" manifests the identity and power of Yahweh. For this reason, his birth day, not Caesar's, is truly good news for all of humankind. He, not Caesar, is Lord and Savior of the world. His reign, not Caesar's, will lead the heavens to erupt in praise of God and the celebration of enduring peace: "Glory to God in the highest heaven, and on earth peace to those whom he favors" (vv. 13–14). This, Luke shows, is how God's plan for the redemption of Israel, and even all of humanity, unfolds. In this peasant infant, not Caesar or any other, divine identity and purpose come into the world and turn it upside down. Thus, already near the start of his narrative, Luke puts Theophilus and the rest of his audience on notice that what God does in Jesus significantly undermines all other claims to mastery over humankind.

There is another dramatic testimony to the sovereign rule of Yahweh in Jesus over against the elite of the Roman world that we should briefly consider. It occurs in Acts 4 as Luke concludes his account of Peter and John's arrest by the Israelite elite and their subsequent release. Inspired by Psalm 2, the believers lift up a celebratory prayer proclaiming that

---

9. Josephus, *Wars*, 6.312–13, cited in Adam Winn, *The Purpose of Mark's Gospel: An Early Christian Response to Roman Imperial Propaganda*, WUNT 245 (Tübingen: Mohr Siebeck, 2008), 161. The Roman historian Titus (*History*, 5.13.1–2) claims that the prophecy is fulfilled by Vespasian and Titus.

all earthly dominion and power pales in comparison to that held by the "Sovereign Lord" and "his Messiah":

> "Sovereign Lord, who made the heaven and the earth, the sea, and everything in them, it is you who said by the Holy Spirit through our ancestor David, your servant:
>
>> 'Why did the Gentiles rage,
>>   and the peoples imagine vain things?
>> The kings of the earth took their stand,
>>   and the rulers have gathered together against the Lord
>>   and against his Messiah.'
>
> For in this city, in fact, both Herod and Pontius Pilate, with the Gentiles and the peoples of Israel, gathered together against your holy servant Jesus, whom you anointed, to do whatever your hand and your plan had predestined to take place. And now, Lord, look at their threats, and grant to your servants to speak your word with all boldness, while you stretch out your hand to heal, and signs and wonders are performed through the name of your holy servant Jesus." (4:24–30)

Luke may not be calling for open insurrection. But he is challenging his recipients' allegiances, urging them to forsake the life carved out for them by "the kings of the earth" and to "speak with all boldness" about life in a new kingdom under a new king with a wildly different set of values they are to make their own (see Acts 4:32–37!). The tide has turned, Luke announces. The social movement Jesus hailed as the "kingdom of God" is already beginning to overtake Caesar's domain. And having turned Theophilus's attention to Psalm 2, the implications ring clear: someday soon, the foundations of Rome and all earthly claims to power—God's messiah "shall break with a rod of iron, and dash in pieces like a potter's vessel!" (Ps 2:8–9). Augustus, Titus, Vespasian, the Judean governors, and the Herods—their claims to sovereignty and beneficence are the source of divine derision and wrath (Ps 2:4–5). God has set God's King on high (Ps 2:6), and "there is salvation in no one else, for there is no other name under heaven or given among mortals by which we must be saved" (Acts 4:12).

ROMANS 12–13

According to some readers of Paul, what seems to be absent from Paul's version of a world gone awry is much attention to concrete, sociopolitical realities. Beyond relatively small groups of detractors that oppose

Paul's teaching in several locales (e.g., Galatia and Corinth), the "enemies" to be overcome are the spiritual corruption of humanity, the vicissitudes of fleshly desire, and the challenges of living together in community (e.g., Rom 7:14–25; 12:1–13; Gal 5:7–26; Phil 3:17–4:1). Paul pays little attention, in other words, to the role of elite rule in thwarting God's desire for God's people, such as we see in other New Testament and Israelite texts like Luke–Acts, Mark, Matthew, Revelation, the Psalms of Solomon, the Maccabean writings, and various apocalyptic traditions. Along somewhat similar lines, Malina draws a sharp distinction between the early Jesus movement as a social movement organization seeking to change Israelite society and counter elite rule, and "post-Jesus groups" whose objectives he claims had notably shifted.

> The Jesus movement was a social movement; his group was a social movement organization. On the other hand, the post-Jesus groups founded by those change agents called "apostles" were not social movement groups since their purpose was not to change "elements of the social structure or reward distribution, or both, of a society." Rather, post-Jesus groups looked to the cosmic rescue of the person, that is the collective selves of the first-century Mediterranean world. For this reason post-Jesus groups were associations most like ancient clubs and *collegia*, equally concerned with the social well-being of collective selves.[10]

Many advocating the view that Paul's focus was on "the cosmic rescue of the person" and the social well-being of collective selves would point to that key moment of transition in Paul's letter to the Romans (12:1–2) as instructive. Here Paul shifts from proclaiming what God has accomplished in Jesus to exhorting the Roman church on how to live out its truth together in community:

> I appeal to you, therefore, brothers and sisters, by the mercies of God, to present your bodies as a living sacrifice, holy and acceptable to God. (v. 1)

Paul will go on to say, "do not be conformed to this world" (v. 2). But his subsequent focus on community life (12:3–15:5) and his encouragement of acquiescence to the governing authorities (13:1–7) seem to reflect a spirit of accommodation toward the dominance of Rome and elite rule. For Paul, according to this view, the battle to be enjoined is primarily a personal and communal one within the confines of the present political order. What likely motivated Paul's accommodating stance toward Roman rule and focus on community life was the expectation that Christ would soon return to right all wrongs (see 1 Thess 4:13–5:11). In short,

---

10. Malina, *New Testament World*, 212.

as apocalyptically shaded, Israelite traditions offering their own telling of the kingdom story in the first century CE, Paul's letters are remarkable for their seeming lack of overt disdain for Roman rule and hope for Rome's impending destruction.

More recently, however, an increasing number of readers of Paul's letters and Romans in particular have emphasized that Paul subtly—yet clearly—counters Roman claims to sovereignty as he celebrates Jesus's exaltation as Lord over creation and the true savior of humankind.[11] Among them, Neil Elliott draws from the distinctions presented by anthropologist James C. Scott between "public transcript," "hidden transcript of the dominant," and the "hidden transcript of the subordinate" to guide his reading of Romans.[12] Elliott endorses Scott's claim that most expressions of protest against domination in antiquity would be introduced into the public transcript only in muted or veiled form, for fear of swift and brutal reprisal: "unable to express their resistance openly, subordinate groups must ordinarily rely on strategies of indirection and disguise, or seek the safety of anonymity."[13] Such indirection and disguise, Elliott among others argues, is precisely what occurs in Paul's letter to the Romans as Paul contrasts the justice of God with "the false claims of mortals who pretend at justice, but deserve God's wrath instead."[14]

As one key example, Elliott asks readers to consider the opening of Romans against a particular setting: the celebration of Nero's ascension to the Roman throne in the public transcript (54 CE), which included the acclamation of heaven and Nero's own deification (recall our discussion of the imperial cult in chapter 2). With these claims and attributions reverberating throughout the Roman Empire and especially within Rome, imagine now how Paul's preface (1:1–4) and what many con-

---

11. N. T. Wright's work reflects this shift in perspective. In "Putting Paul Together Again: Toward a Synthesis of Paul's Theology," in *Paul's Theology: Volume 1, Thessalonians, Philippians, Galatians, Philemon*, ed. Jouette Basler (Minneapolis: Fortress Press, 1991), 200, Wright argued that "the salvation Paul expects is not from an external enemy (namely, Rome or 'the Kittim') but from the wrath of God (1 Thess 1:10, etc.). Evil is not 'out there' in the world beyond the pale of ethnic covenant membership, but a matter of the *kardía*." A little more than a decade later, in *The Resurrection of the Son of God* (Minneapolis: Fortress Press, 2003), 728–29, Wright expressed the implications of Paul's proclamation of Jesus as resurrected son of God in relation to Rome in much different terms: "Calling Jesus 'son of god' within this context of meaning, [early Christian communities] constituted themselves by implication as a collection of rebel cells within Caesar's empire, loyal to a different monarch, a different *kyrios*. Saying 'Jesus has been raised from the dead' proved to be self-involving in that it gained its meaning within this counter-imperial worldview."

12. Neil Elliott, *The Arrogance of the Nations: Reading Romans in the Shadow of Empire*, Paul in Critical Contexts (Minneapolis: Fortress Press, 2008), 30–57. James C. Scott, *Domination and the Arts of Resistance: Hidden Transcripts* (New Haven: Yale University Press, 1992).

13. Scott, *Domination*, 5.

14. Elliott, *Arrogance of the Nations*, 62.

sider the topic sentence, or thesis of the letter (1:16–17) would have been heard by Paul's first recipients in Rome. In contrast and in resistance to the presentation of Nero as the king who arrives with proper pedigree and divine approval, Paul crafts a sender formula that "resonates with the weight of Roman diplomatic vocabulary"[15] and announces (following Elliott's translation):

> Paul, slave of the Messiah Jesus, called as an apostle set apart to the proclamation of God's triumph, which he proclaimed beforehand through his prophets in the holy scriptures, concerning his son, the descendant of the seed of David, according to the flesh, appointed God's son in power according to the spirit of holiness by resurrection from the dead: Jesus, the Messiah, our Lord . . . (1:1–4).[16]

Moreover, as the opening of the letter moves to its stated focus, Paul announces his "eagerness to proclaim the gospel to you also who are in Rome" (v. 15). He follows with a synopsis of the gospel's essential core in a chain of subordinating conjunctions (Elliott's translation):

> for I am not ashamed to announce God's imminent triumph [*euangelion*]; for his proclamation is the power of God for salvation to all who are faithful, to the Jew first and also to the Greek; for in it the justice of God is revealed, through faithfulness, to faithfulness; as it is written, "The one who is just shall live by faithfulness"; for the wrath of God is revealed from heaven against all impiety and injustice of those who by their injustice suppress truth . . . (Rom 1:16–18).[17]

Paul, according to Elliott, is announcing that God's triumph is unveiled in Jesus's triumph over all earthly lords and claims to sovereignty over creation. The one whose victory Paul exclaims in subtle though recognizable implication is Jesus, not Nero. The deification endorsed by heaven, which rightly commands human devotion and faithfulness, is not that of the emperor but of Yahweh's Messiah.[18]

Thus when Paul calls upon the Roman believers in 12:1–2 to no longer be conformed to this world but be transformed by the renewing of their minds, he is urging them to set aside any allegiances they may still cultivate toward Rome and Roman ways. In place of that allegiance to Rome—and in contrast to Roman values—Paul exhorts believers to devote themselves to the "good, acceptable and perfect" way of God, as

---

15. Elliott, *Arrogance of the Nations*, 63.
16. Elliott, *Arrogance of the Nations*, 62.
17. Elliott, *Arrogance of the Nations*, 74.
18. So also Wright, *The Resurrection of the Son of God*, 729.

they live in humble fellowship with one another under the lordship of Christ (vv. 3–8).

How then are we to understand the accommodating tone of Paul's instruction to be subject to the governing authorities shortly to follow in Romans 13? Those who find in the epistle subtle yet sharp polemic against Rome have generally adopted one of three ways of accounting for these verses. One is to point to recent disturbances in both Rome and the diaspora that indicate the volatile situation in the capital city while the letter was being written. Paul's words of submission and accommodation are meant to avoid further bloodshed and reprisals as the Roman leadership seeks to reestablish its control.[19] Another, as promoted by Robert Jewett, is to make the case that Paul's language in Romans 13 actually presents a subtle yet recognizable critique of Roman rule in that it calls for a willing subordination rather than a forced obedience. It also challenges the hierarchy of Rome by calling for *all* persons to subject themselves to the authorities regardless of citizenship or social rank.[20] A third option is offered by T. L. Carter who argues that Paul's use of such gratuitously deferential language would have clearly signaled to members of the Roman church that his remarks were meant to be understood as ironic, or sarcastic.[21]

These three explanations need not be seen as mutually exclusive. Instead, one could argue that Paul calls for submission here in order to avoid devastating reprisal while using both subtle and sarcastic language that would nevertheless undermine Rome's own claim to sovereignty and divine acclamation. After all, in the immediately preceding verses, Paul refers to persecution and suffering as one of the evils believers presently experience under the reign of these very same authorities! The response he calls believers to adopt is to "bless those who persecute you and do not curse them" (12:14) and to be those who "overcome evil with good" (12:21). Even so, Paul's instruction also betrays an edge of disdain and judgment: believers are to "leave room for the wrath of God; for it is written, 'Vengeance is mine, I will repay says the Lord'" (12:19). Even the believers' irreproachable goodness "will heap burning coals on their heads" (12:21). In sum, by repeatedly—though indirectly and subtly—challenging the ideology of Rome, Paul calls upon believers and believing communities to adopt ways of thinking and relating that manifest *God's* way and rule. Believers are to resist as much as prudence allows, bearing witness to the true Lord and kingdom. And as they do

19. See Elliott, *Arrogance of the Nations*, 154.

20. Robert Jewett, *Romans: A Commentary*, Hermeneia (Minneapolis: Fortress Press, 2007), 787–90.

21. T. L. Carter, "The Irony of Romans 13," *NovT* 46 (2004): 209–28.

so, they are to hold on to the hope that ultimate vengeance belongs to God, and the final outcome for those in Christ is not in doubt.

In my view, Elliott and others help us appreciate Paul's implicit (though likely obvious to Paul's original recipients) challenge to Roman claims of sovereignty and divine approval, and many Roman values. At the same time, one can push the pendulum too far to the other side, focusing only on Paul's anti-imperial agenda and neglect Paul's equally fundamental concern for the way in which sin and death have taken up residence in human communities of any size *and* in individual human souls. The transformation Paul urges and celebrates is plural and singular in person; it is cosmic and personal in scope. The implications of the coming of God's reign for Rome and other embodiments of evil throughout the cosmos also bear upon the heart of every member of the human race. For Paul, *wherever* evil is found, there God's grace will be countering and conquering.

If this reading of Romans 13 is close to the mark, then care must be taken when applying the anthropological models of social movement and countermovement to "stages" of the early Christian community, as useful as those categories may be. As noted above, Malina and others see a shift from the early Jesus movement as social movement to the early church as stabilizing fictive kin groups with a communal focus. Without denying the possibility of those tendencies to some degree and in some settings, I think that the development of early Christian communities cannot be so uniformly categorized. We still find a lot of social movement sentiment coursing through the writings of the New Testament, including those (in the case of the gospels and Revelation) coming to their final form during the last quarter of the first century! The danger of categories is that they can facilitate false dichotomies if not utilized judiciously, and I think that may be the case with the too-neat classification that Malina and others offer. I would also question the assumption informing these models, that such communities nearly always progress in stages from one type of community to another. Rather, it may be that the exigencies of the time, or the identity and social locations of leaders within the community at the present moment, or still other factors, determine the character of the community's relationship to the wider society just as much, if not more than, any tendency in group development. The true character of the early Christian communities, in other words, may be more volatile and variable than a simple model of consistent, linear stages of development can adequately capture. And as Professor Malina himself would often say during the discussions of the CBA Social Scientific Task Force, "If a model doesn't fit, then change it!"

TEXTS OF CONFORMITY

1 TIMOTHY 2:8–15 AND 1 CORINTHIANS 14:33B–36

This is not to say, however, that the drive for social stability and even countermovement is not well represented among the biblical texts. Indeed it is. To illustrate the diversity we can find within the New Testament writings in terms of resistance and conformity to larger Mediterranean culture advocated by early Christian communities, let's turn to two New Testament passages that reassert traditional Mediterranean roles for women within the Christian community.

[8] I desire, then, that in every place the men should pray, lifting up holy hands without anger or argument; [9] also that the women should dress themselves modestly and decently in suitable clothing, not with their hair braided, or with gold, pearls, or expensive clothes, [10] but with good works, as is proper for women who profess reverence for God. [11] Let a woman learn in silence with full submission. [12] I permit no woman to teach or to have authority over a man; she is to keep silent. [13] For Adam was formed first, then Eve; [14] and Adam was not deceived, but the woman was deceived and became a transgressor. [15] Yet she will be saved through childbearing, provided they continue in faith and love and holiness, with modesty.

[33b] As in all the churches of the saints, [34] women should be silent in the churches. For they are not permitted to speak, but should be subordinate, as the law also says. [35] If there is anything they desire to know, let them ask their husbands at home. For it is shameful for a woman to speak in church. [36] Or did the word of God originate with you? Or are you the only ones it has reached?

There have been numerous attempts by modern interpreters to soften these injunctions severely limiting the participation of women in Christian communities. But for our purposes it is important to note the rhetorical energy and force invested in these prohibitions: "I permit *no* woman to teach or have authority over a man." "It is *shameful* for a woman to speak in church." "As in *all the churches of the saints*, women should be silent in the churches." Moreover, the writer of 1 Timothy grounds the rationale for his instruction in the narrative of Genesis 2–3: "For Adam was formed first, then Eve; and Adam was not deceived, but the woman was deceived and became a transgressor" (v. 14).[22]

22. Ironically, this misogynist reading of Genesis 2 ("For Adam was formed first . . .") fails to appreciate the extremely countercultural character of this creation story. The structure, character speech, and repetition of the account of the woman's creation emphasize the *sameness* of

The vehemence implied by these statements indicates the likelihood that women were in fact speaking and assuming leadership roles within their early Christian communities. Other New Testament texts affirm this was likely the case: women actively prophesied (e.g., Luke 2:36–38 [Anna]; Acts 2:17–18; 21:9 [Philip's daughters]; 1 Cor 11:5), taught or evangelized as Paul's "coworkers" (e.g., Acts 18:26; Rom 16:3 [Priscilla]; Phil 4:2–3 [Euodia and Syntyche]), or served in positions of leadership (e.g., Rom 16:1–2 [Phoebe]). This development among early Christian communities, of recognizing and valuing the testimony and leadership of women, clearly transgresses the gender roles typical of Mediterranean culture in which maleness was the ideal and femaleness was often denigrated (see chapter 3). This tendency to embolden women to serve in these roles is one of several features marking early Christian communities as social movements. However, as 1 Timothy 2 and 1 Corinthians 14 clearly indicate, not all within these early Christian communities were comfortable with the eschewal of social convention when it came to women.

Did Paul himself change his mind on the place of women in the community? This is possible. But most scholars understand 1 Timothy to be written in Paul's name well after his death. He likely did not author 1 Timothy 2:8–15. How then are we to make sense of 1 Corinthians 14:34–35? One plausible explanation is that these verses were a secondary insertion. Verses 34–35 are found after verse 40 in several early manuscripts. Coupled with the reality that they express a perspective on women that is difficult to reconcile with Paul's commendation of female apostles, teachers, and deacons elsewhere in his letters, the transient nature of verses 34–35 suggests that Paul did not compose them,

---

the man and woman's respective natures and the complementary character of their identity and calling ("This at last is bone of my bones . . . [2:23]; "one flesh" [v. 24]), not the subservience of woman to man. When "helper" (*ezer*) is seen against the broader background of how that term is used throughout the Old Testament (mostly in reference to God!), it identifies the woman in this context as one who can provide assistance for the man that he is not able to provide for himself (see v. 20). As for Adam being first, that too does not appear to be of interest to the writer of Genesis 2. In fact, Adam's act of naming himself as "man" and his partner as "woman" (v. 23b) indicates the biblical writer's recognition that gender becomes part of the human experience only when the woman is created. Meanwhile, subservience of woman to man enters into creation not here, but later and as a consequence of humanity's sin (see 3:16). The notion that the first sin is the responsibility of woman alone is difficult to reconcile with Genesis 3. The text implies that Adam was with the woman during her twisted conversation with the serpent and readily accepted the forbidden fruit from her hand (3:6). Note too that Adam's excuse in verse 12 can hardly be seen as credible, since he blames both the woman *and* God for his transgression: "The woman who you gave to be with me . . ." (v. 12). I also think it doubtful that Paul would concur with the writer of 1 Timothy 2 on the origin of human sin: Paul emphasizes that sin came into the world through Adam, who in this context Paul likely views as representative of humanity in general (see Rom 5:12–21).

but they were added later to his letter as part of a countermovement against the emergence of female leaders in the early church.[23]

Acts and Paul's letters (especially Galatians) tell us that the inclusion of non-Israelites—without requiring them to adopt traditional identity markers of Judaism (circumcision and purity practices)—was another social movement resisted by some within early Christian communities (see Acts 15). Along with the texts from 1 Timothy and 1 Corinthians we just considered, these accounts of disagreement among early Christians over important social issues reveal that countermovements existed among them, at least with respect to some elements of their community life. Paying attention to these social and political dynamics at work among early believers helps us account for the diversity of perspectives on these topics we find among early Christians, and even within the New Testament.

CONTROVERSY AMONG ISRAELITES OVER THE INCLUSION OF GENTILES

Preserved within several Old Testament traditions is testimony to a major controversy that embroiled Israelites in conflict during the early Second Temple Period. Not only do these traditions bear witness to this controversy, they also participate in it. On one side you have the writer(s) of Ezra and Nehemiah, and on the other you have the writers of Third Isaiah, Ruth, Jonah, and even Malachi.

First, a little background to set the stage for this controversy. In the late sixth century BCE, King Zedekiah of Judah made the brash and foolish move of rebelling against Israel's Babylonian overlords. In 587, the Babylonian armies invaded and eventually leveled the city of Jerusalem and surrounding towns, killing many of the inhabitants, razing the temple, and taking most of the survivors, including the now eyeless king Zedekiah, back to Babylon. Suddenly, nearly everything that defined Israel as a nation and people was gone: land, holy city, temple, monarchy. During their time in exile, the surviving Israelites reflected on their experience guided by their sacred traditions and several of the prophets. They came to realize first of all that the tragedy of destruc-

---

23. Should these statements be regarded as original to Paul, Barbara E. Reid (*Wisdom's Feast: An Invitation to Feminist Interpretation of the Scriptures* [Eerdmans: Grand Rapids, 2016] 109–10) offers another plausible explanation of these prohibitions against women that are in clear conflict with Paul's commendation of women elsewhere. As we see in other sections of the Corinthian correspondence (e.g., 1 Cor 6:12–13, 8:4), Paul is actually quoting statements made by some of the Corinthians themselves in vv. 33b–35, and v. 36 is his rejoinder showing his rejection of this line of thinking.

tion and exile was a result of their unrelenting sin against God and one another. They also came to believe that, despite all appearances, God still cared deeply for them and would one day restore them. The book of Ezra tells the story about the Israelite people in Jerusalem after they were allowed by King Cyrus of Persia to return to their homeland (539), including the rebuilding of the temple and the people's recommitment to following God's Torah. Despite a delay in the reconstruction of the temple—a seventeen-year hiatus due to problems caused by their enemies in the north—and the numerous hardships the people faced, it must have been for many an exciting time. Many likely saw in these events the hand of God at work, moving the people closer to that glorious restoration of Jerusalem promised by the prophets.

COUNTERMOVEMENT: EZRA AND NEHEMIAH

Some years after the temple was completed and rededicated, still other Israelites, including the scribe Ezra and the heads of many leading families, returned to Jerusalem with the blessing of the Persian king, Artaxerxes. Ezra is celebrated by the biblical writer as a "scribe skilled in the law of Moses that the Lord the God of Israel had given; and the king granted him all that he asked, for the hand of the Lord his God was upon him" (Ezra 7:6). Soon after he arrives, however, Ezra is confronted with disturbing news. Many Israelites, including priests, Levites, and officials, have taken non-Israelite wives. In the words of the officials, "the holy seed has mixed itself with the peoples of the lands" (9:1–2). Ezra rends his garments, pulls hair from his head and beard, and leads the people in an impassioned prayer of confession (Ezra 9:6–15). Ezra praises God for allowing them to return to the devastated city. It was more than they deserved, for "from the days of our ancestors to this day, we have been deep in guilt, and for our iniquities we, our kings, and our priests have been handed over to the kings of the lands, to the sword, to captivity, to plundering, and to utter shame, as is now the case" (v. 8). With great anguish he acknowledges that they have once again broken God's law, for God has commanded them concerning the peoples of the land "not to give daughters to their sons, neither take daughters for their sons, and never seek their peace and prosperity" (v. 12). He begs for God's forgiveness, lest God bring destruction upon them once again. Shecaniah, son of Jehiel, steps forward to address Ezra and proposes a remedy: "let us make a covenant with our God to send away all these wives and their children, according to the counsel of my lord and of those who tremble at the commandment of our God. Take action, for it is your duty, and we are with you. Be strong, and do it!" (10:3–4). Ezra stands and makes all of Israel swear that they would do as had been said (v. 5). While Ezra continues to fast, still "mourning over the faithlessness of the exiles," word was sent out throughout Jerusalem and Judah for all to assemble in the Holy City. Those who failed to comply would lose their ancestral landholding and themselves be banished from Israel (v. 8). After a delay due to heavy rains (or the foot-dragging resistance of some?), a census is taken to determine who had transgressed the law, and who must go. Then the non-Israelite women and their children are sent away (v. 44).

The book of Nehemiah is believed by most scholars to have been written by the same author who produced Ezra, and the two books were likely created as a single volume. The figure Nehemiah, who became governor in Judea, may have been a contemporary of Ezra (as the narrative implies) or may have arrived at a time shortly after Ezra. One of the main features of the author's portrayal of these two leaders is the complementary character of their respective tenures. Accordingly, Nehemiah's policy on relations with non-Israelites parallels that of Ezra:

> On that day they read from the book of Moses in the hearing of the people; and in it was found written that no Ammonite or Moabite should ever enter the assembly of God, because they did not meet the Israelites with bread and water, but hired Balaam against them to curse them—yet our God turned the curse into a blessing. When the people heard the law, they separated from Israel all those of foreign descent. (Neh 13:1–3)

Later on in the same chapter (vv. 23–27), Nehemiah also condemns mixed marriages between Israelites and non-Israelites with words as uncompromising as we find in Ezra:

> In those days also I saw Jews who had married women of Ashdod, Ammon, and Moab; and half of their children spoke the language of Ashdod, and they could not speak the language of Judah, but spoke the language of various peoples. And I contended with them and cursed them and beat some of them and pulled out their hair; and I made them take an oath in the name of God, saying, "You shall not give your daughters to their sons, or take their daughters for your sons or for yourselves. Did not King Solomon of Israel sin on account of such women? Among the many nations there was no king like him, and he was beloved by his God, and God made him king over all Israel; nevertheless, foreign women made even him to sin. Shall we then listen to you and do all this great evil and act treacherously against our God by marrying foreign women?"

The closing of the book follows, with Nehemiah offering a summary of the work that he has accomplished, beginning with, "Thus I cleansed them from everything foreign" (v. 30), and concluding with the petition, "Remember me, O my God, for good" (v. 31).

The "good" that the biblical author believed Nehemiah and Ezra were accomplishing in cleansing Israel from all that was foreign is based upon Torah traditions found in the Pentateuch. When renewing the covenant with Israel following the golden calf affair (Exod 34:11–35), God instructs the people to avoid the inhabitants of the land that God is going to give to them. They are not to make a covenant with them, lest they be led astray to worship their gods and take wives from among them (vv. 11–16). In Deuteronomy 7:1–6, with Israel on the verge of entering the promised land, Moses gives these commands concerning the Gentiles they will encounter:

> when the LORD your God gives them over to you and you defeat them, then you must utterly destroy them. Make no covenant with them and show them no mercy. Do not intermarry with them, giving your daughters to their sons or taking their daughters for your sons, for that would turn away your children from following me, to serve other gods. Then the anger of the LORD would be kindled against you, and he would destroy you quickly. (vv. 2–4)

Later in Deuteronomy, Moses orders Israel:

> But as for the towns of these peoples that the LORD your God is giving you as an inheritance, you must not let anything that breathes remain alive. You shall annihilate them—the Hittites and the Amorites, the Canaanites and the Perizzites, the Hivites and the Jebusites—just as the LORD your God has commanded, so that they may not teach you to do all the abhorrent things that they do for their gods, and you thus sin against the LORD your God. (20:16–18)

The motivation consistently given for Israel's need to avoid the Gentiles in these and similar passages is the fear that Gentiles will lead Israel astray to worship other gods. Thus the peoples of the land are to be avoided at all costs, even at the cost of their very existence. We find this exterminatory policy put into practice during Israel's conquest of the promised land (see Josh 11:16–20). The "cleansing" that Ezra and Nehemiah pursued, while different in its method—divorce, deportation, and compulsory oaths of obedience to these Torah commands—had the same objective of maintaining the ethnic and covenantal purity of Israel, what some refer to as "genealogical purity." These countermovements under Ezra and Nehemiah challenged what they saw as the illicit shifting of boundaries defining who could belong to true Israel. While the cleansing Ezra and Nehemiah advocated may not have been genocidal, it was likely deadly, at least eventually so, for many of those women and children who were "set aside." As widows and orphans unconnected to male providers, their prospects for sustainable sustenance were bleak. Perhaps some of these foreign women were able to reconnect with their families of origin. Perhaps some were received by villages in the area. But many were likely left to a desperate and short-term existence.

SOCIAL MOVEMENT: VOICES OF RESISTANCE

The policies enacted and enforced by Ezra and Nehemiah, however, do not exhaust the perspectives provided by the writers and compilers of the Israelite Scriptures on the matter of non-Israelites. Long before this controversy erupts, we also find within the biblical writings a much more inclusive, even welcoming, stream of tradition. Gentiles have been included among God's people since the time of the Exodus ("a mixed crowd also went up with them," Exod 12:38). Commonly referred to as "aliens," they are also called to abide by many of the commandments of the law (Lev 17:12; 18:26; 24:22; Num 9:14; 15:11–16; Deut 5:14; cf. 1 Kings 8:41–43). By following Yahweh's Torah, aliens are called to participate in Israel's covenantal identity, since God's law is given to Israel to set them apart from the nations and mold them into God's special possession (Exod 19:1–6). In addition, and in sharp contrast to the exterminatory policies enacted later, Israel is repeatedly called upon to provide for the aliens living among them (e.g., Lev 19:10, 33–34; 23:22; Deut 24:17–21; Jer 22:3; Ezek 22:29). Moreover, Moses himself takes a Midianite wife, and his father-in-law, Jethro, provides his inexperienced son-in-law with sage advice (Exod 3:1; 18:1–27).

One could argue that such positive regard for non-Israelites was to be granted to only those aliens who joined God's people prior to their entrance into the land. Because they did not pose a threat to Israel's religious fidelity, they were not singled out for exclusion as were the "peoples of the land." However, Gentiles from among the "peoples of the land" play key roles in the history of God's people after the conquest begins. Rahab the prostitute shelters and saves the lives of those sent to spy out the land in Joshua 2. She professes faith in Yahweh: "The Lord your God is indeed God in the heaven above and on earth below" (Josh 2:11). In return for her kindness and faith, her and her family's lives are spared. Thus, enmeshed in the very account of Israel's conquest of Canaan and the slaughter of its Gentile inhabitants lest they lead God's people into sin, stands the story of a God-fearing Gentile woman (a prostitute no less!) who facilitates Israel's entrance into the promised land.

Ruth

The story of Rahab is thick with irony, but it gets thicker with the story of Ruth. Ruth is a Moabite woman and thus non-Israelite (recall Nehemiah's particular disdain for Moabites). Ruth marries into an Israelite family from Bethlehem that settled in Moab, consisting of two sons and their widowed mother, Naomi. After both of Naomi's sons die (including Ruth's husband), Naomi prepares to leave Moab and her widowed daughters-in-law, Orpah and Ruth, and return to Judah. She instructs Orpah and Ruth to remain in the land and return to their own relatives. Orpah heeds Naomi's words and bids farewell. But Ruth clings to Naomi. Once again Naomi urges her to depart: "See, your sister-in-law has gone back to her people and to her gods; return after your sister-in-law." But Ruth will not be dissuaded. In response, she proclaims these now famous words (1:16–17):

> "Do not press me to leave you or to turn back from following you! Where you go, I will go; where you lodge, I will lodge; your people shall be my people, and your God my God. Where you die, I will die—there will I be buried. May the LORD do thus and so to me, and more as well, if even death parts me from you!"

What makes these words especially poignant is not simply the fact that this happens to be a moving scene, filled with pathos. Many scholars conclude, based on its genre and style of writing, that the story of Ruth was written down some time after the exile. Consider what this means. Around the very same time many were following Ezra and Nehemiah's exclusionary policies, including the biblical author of Ezra-Nehemiah as he was approvingly penning his account, some other Israelite writer was recording the story of Ruth, shaping it and using language that was sure to catch the ear of his fellow Israelites. So imagine that you are an Israelite scribe with the unhappy duty of reading this newly composed story of Ruth in the house of the Judean governor, in the mid-fifth century BCE, to a group that includes Ezra, Nehemiah, and the leading officials of the restored Jerusalem. Imagine their reaction to the story as it unfolds, their discomfort with the statement that Naomi's Israelite sons "took Moabite wives." Imagine their approval when Naomi commands Ruth, the Moabite, to turn away from her and instead follow her sister-in-law "who has gone back to her people and to her gods." Imagine their surprise and dismay when Ruth again refuses to leave, and instead announces, "your people shall be my people, and your God my God." And imagine their growing discomfort, furor, and even perhaps dissonance as these members of the Israelite countermovement elite hear how the rest of the story unfolds. They hear that the obstinate, non-Israelite, Moabite Ruth once again marries, and once again to an upstanding Israelite man, Boaz. They hear that this mixed couple bears a son. His name is Obed. And by now, they likely begin to remember that Obed becomes the father of Jesse, who becomes the father of a ruddy-looking youth, highly gifted with a slingshot. That's right, they remember that the Moabite Ruth is the great-grandmother of the great King David, whose "holy seed" Ezra, Nehemiah, and the leading officials are hoping will one day return to the throne of Israel!

Isaiah

The writer of Ruth was not alone. The oracles found in the later chapters of Isaiah are dated by most scholars to the same period as Ezra and Nehemiah. With expression both eloquent and moving, Isaiah 56:1–8 proclaims that all those who devote themselves to Yahweh, even those who were formerly excluded from the people of Israel—foreigners and the genitally deformed (in this case, eunuchs; see Deut 23:1)—are now to be welcomed among God's people.

> [1] Thus says the LORD: Maintain justice, and do what is right,
>   for soon my salvation will come,
>   and my deliverance be revealed.
> [2] Happy is the mortal who does this, the one who holds it fast,
>   who keeps the sabbath, not profaning it,
>   and refrains from doing any evil.
> [3] Do not let the foreigner joined to the LORD say,
>   "The LORD will surely separate me from his people";
> and do not let the eunuch say,
>   "I am just a dry tree."
> [4] For thus says the LORD:
> To the eunuchs who keep my sabbaths,
>   who choose the things that please me
>   and hold fast my covenant,
> [5] I will give, in my house and within my walls,
>   a monument and a name better than sons and daughters;
> I will give them an everlasting name
>   that shall not be cut off.

⁶ And the foreigners who join themselves to the LORD,
    to minister to him, to love the name of the LORD,
    and to be his servants,
all who keep the sabbath, and do not profane it,
    and hold fast my covenant—
⁷ these I will bring to my holy mountain,
    and make them joyful in my house of prayer;
their burnt offerings and their sacrifices
    will be accepted on my altar;
for my house shall be called a house of prayer
    for all peoples.
⁸ Thus says the Lord GOD,
    who gathers the outcasts of Israel,
I will gather others to them
    besides those already gathered.

Note how the language employed by the prophet or group producing these oracles invites us to hear its instruction with Ezra and Nehemiah's practices in mind: "Do not let the foreigner joined to the Lord say, 'The Lord will surely *separate* me from his people." Here the Hebrew verb for "separate" (*badal*) is the same as that used in Ezra 10:11 in reference to the Israelites separating themselves from foreign wives and their children, and in Nehemiah 13:3 in reference to their separation from all those of foreign descent. Verse 8 strengthens the likelihood of an intended connection as it specifically holds in view the congregation of returned exiles and those "others"—namely, the foreigners and eunuchs—whom God will gather to join them: "Thus says the Lord God, who *gathers the outcasts of Israel*, I will *gather others to them besides those already gathered*. Note too the all-encompassing embrace God offers to faithful foreigners: "these I will bring to my holy mountain and make them joyful in my house of prayer; their burnt offerings and their sacrifices will be accepted on my altar" (v. 7). They are to fully partake in the life of God's people. Placed in the mouth of the eighth-century prophet Isaiah, this oracle announces that God's plan for a restored Israel does not fit the exclusion of an earlier age, or the exclusion some are advocating in the present age. Yahweh announces that "my house shall be a house of prayer for all peoples." According to the framers of these oracles, that time has now come: "Thus says the Lord: Maintain justice and do what is right" (v. 1).

Malachi

Malachi is another postexilic, prophetic text offering instruction that is often viewed by scholars in connection with the exclusionary policies of Ezra and Nehemiah. However, most scholars argue that like Ezra and Nehemiah, Malachi condemns mixed marriages in 2:10–12 when he chastises Judah for profaning the sanctuary and "marrying the daughter of a foreign god" (v. 11). Yet the phrase "marrying the daughter of a foreign god" need not refer to the practice of Israelites marrying foreign women. Instead, it may refer simply to idolatrous activity in general. I believe that if we suspend the assumption that 2:10–12 condemns mixed marriages between Israelites and Gentiles, we find that numerous features of the text instead suggest that Malachi is actually defending these mixed marriages and condemning the marital policies of Ezra and Nehemiah.

Let's begin with what comes immediately following this phrase in 2:10–12. In 2:13–16, the prophet rails against divorce. Malachi is the only prophet to address the issue, and what seems apparent from the prophet's rebuke is that the practice had become rather widespread during this time.

> [13] And this you do as well: You cover the LORD's altar with tears, with weeping and groaning because he no longer regards the offering or accepts it with favor at your hand. [14] You ask, "Why does he not?" Because the LORD was a witness between you and the wife of your youth, to whom you have been faithless, though she is your companion and your wife by covenant. [15] Did not one God make her? Both flesh and spirit are his. And what does the one God desire? Godly offspring. So look to yourselves, and do not let anyone be faithless to the wife of his youth. [16] For I hate divorce, says the LORD, the God of Israel, and covering one's garment with violence, says the LORD of hosts. So take heed to yourselves and do not be faithless.

If we read these verses with the policies of Ezra and Nehemiah in mind, without assuming that the phrase "marrying the daughter of a foreign god" in verse 11 refers to Israelites marrying Gentiles, the possibility that Malachi is instead supporting those mixed marriages and condemning the marital policies of Ezra and Nehemiah presents itself. Twice the prophet rebukes those who have been unfaithful to "the wife of your youth," as if to say "You know, that wife to whom you were first married and with whom you had children." The concern for "godly offspring" underscores the destructive and tragic consequences of divorce. The children who have been sent away are not only dishonored, they have been sent away from the people who are charged with the task of guiding them in the ways of God. The phrase, "covering one's garment with violence," may refer to the rather heartless manner in which the wives and children were cast out and the desperation they will likely suffer as widows and orphans.

Moreover, if Malachi was condemning mixed marriages in verses 10–12, then it would seem counterproductive for him to immediately condemn divorce in the strongest possible terms: "For I hate divorce, says the Lord, the God of Israel" (v. 16), when divorce was the very means being used by the returned exiles to rectify that "sin." Some scholars attempt to resolve this problem by arguing that the returned exiles must have been divorcing their Israelite wives in order to marry foreign women, and that is why Malachi condemns both mixed marriage and divorce. However, there is nothing in the writings of this era to support this theory. In fact, if this was a common occurrence among postexilic Israelites, then it surely would have been raised by Ezra and Nehemiah as yet another reason for condemning mixed marriages. But they never hint that Israelites were divorcing their Israelite wives in order to marry foreign women. The problem as the author of Ezra-Nehemiah describes it is that many of the returned exiles were simply marrying foreign women *instead of* Israelite women. Accordingly, Ezra and Nehemiah do not condemn divorce; they advocate it in this instance as a means of dissolving the mixed marriages.

Equally revealing is the focus and development of the text leading up to 2:10–12. At first glance these verses may seem simply to address the problem of priests bringing blemished or less-than-desirable offerings to God. But there is more going on here. Let's zero in on 1:8–12:

> [8] When you offer blind animals in sacrifice, is that not wrong? And when you offer those that are lame or sick, is that not wrong? Try presenting that to your governor; will he be pleased with you or show you favor? says the LORD of hosts. [9] And now implore the favor of God, that he may be gracious to us. The fault is yours. Will he show favor to any of you? says the LORD of hosts. [10] Oh, that someone among you would shut the temple doors, so that you would not kindle fire on my altar in vain! I have no pleasure in you, says the LORD of hosts, and I will not accept an offering from your hands. [11] For from the rising of the sun to its setting my name is great among the nations, and in every place incense is offered to my name, and a pure offering; for my name is great among the nations, says the LORD of hosts. [12] But you profane it when you say that the Lord's table is polluted, and the food for it may be despised.

Notice the reference to seeking the governor's (Nehemiah's?) favor in verse 8, and how that is contrasted with the more important task of imploring the favor of *God* (v. 9), inviting us to see in Malachi's words a critique of cultic practices endorsed by the present leadership. But the Lord takes no pleasure in their vain sacrifices and wishes that the doors of the temple were closed (v. 10). Why? In giving his explanation, the prophet not only cites unworthy offerings (vv. 7–8, 13–14) but also sets up a contrast between two different groups of worshippers. This is an important development, and it helps us to see an additional dimension of the prophet's rebuke. The prophet explains that in contrast to the worship of the returned exiles, God's name is held in great honor by many from among the nations, and praised with pure offerings in every place (v. 11). In other words, there are many—including *Gentiles* presumably—besides the returned exiles calling upon and praising the name of the Lord and, in fact, *they* are doing a much better job of it (see also v. 14).

Thus what the prophet rails against in chapter 1 is the infidelity of Israel's worship marked by (1) the offering of polluted foods (i.e., from animals that are lame, sick, or "taken by violence") *in contrast to* the faithful in other nations who rightly praise and worship God; and (2) an attitude that seems more concerned with the favor of the governor than the favor of Yahweh. The prophet is clearly not, in these verses, endorsing the status quo guarded by the Israelite leadership. This becomes even clearer in 2:1–3 as the prophet rebukes the priesthood in a most degrading fashion: if they persist in their unfaithfulness, the dung of their offerings will be spread upon their faces! (v. 3) Two additional features of Malachi's rebuke are important for us to note as well. In 2:4–9, the prophet goes on to compare the current priesthood with Levi, the ancestor of all priests (2:4–9). They are so unlike him. They have turned aside from his pure and upright ways, and the ways of God. How? "*They have shown partiality*" in their instruction and administration of the temple (v. 9). Still later, Malachi includes "those who thrust aside the alien" as among those who will be subject to God's judgment (3:5).

In sum, Malachi's rebuke of the returned exiles displays a positive orientation toward the worship of Yahweh by non-Israelites, a rejection of the partiality displayed by the temple leadership, and an urgent reminder to care for the alien among them. These features of the text, coupled with the prophet's scathing rebuke of divorce, hardly cohere with the genealogical purity and exclusive marital policies endorsed by Ezra and Nehemiah. Furthermore, turn again to 2:10 and note how the words "Have we not all one father? Has not one God created us?" now ring clear. Many scholars suggest that the pronouns "we" and "us" in these phrases refer only to the people of Israel. But given the favorable regard of non-Israelites evident in the immediate context and the rebuke against the priests' partiality that comes immediately before the statement, a far more inclusive reading is warranted. In asking, "Have we not all one father? Has not one God created us?" Malachi, like the writers of Ruth and Isaiah 56, exhorts his brethren to broaden their own conceptions of who is to be included among God's people: are we not all—including Gentiles—children of God? he asks. Similarly, in his castigation of divorce that follows, the prophet says concerning the wives being sent away, "Did not one God make her? Both flesh and Spirit are his" (2:15).

Therefore, when the prophet refers to the profaning of the covenant and sanctuary again in 2:10–12, he likely has in view the current policy of exclusion and divorce perpetrated by the returned exiles against non-Jews who, in the prophet's mind, have proven faithful in their worship of Yahweh. Then, with a sarcastic and penetrating twist of irony, the prophet boldly claims that it is the exclusionary attitudes and the substandard worship practices of the returned exiles that are, in fact, the stuff of idolatry. You are worried about Israel being led astray to worship idols because some are taking non-Jewish wives? He (in effect) says, when you—*Judah*—reject those who in contrast to yourselves rightly worship God, then *you* are the ones acting as those married to a daughter of a foreign god! This must stop. For you are the ones who will be cut off if you persist in this most unfaithful treatment of God's beloved and God's sanctuary (v. 12). Then, fittingly, follows the prophet's condemnation of divorce: "And you do this as well . . ." (v. 13).

Jonah

There is still another witness left to consider: the book of Jonah. Although scholars have struggled to date the work, and thus we cannot with confidence assign it to the postexilic period, it still provides yet another example of an Israelite perspective toward Gentiles that is in sharp contrast to that of the author of Ezra-Nehemiah and other Old Testament traditions. You know the story. The prophet Jonah is told by God to go at once to Nineveh: to "cry out against it; for their wickedness has come up before me" (1:2). Jonah's reluctance to go is certainly understandable. Set in the eighth century BCE, Nineveh is the great city of the Assyrian Empire, the despised and feared enemy of Israel. So Jonah takes his chances, and runs from God. After a nasty storm at sea, an equally nasty ride in the belly of a fish, and a violent regurgitation, Jonah finds himself on dry land with a renewed—though still reluctant—willingness to listen to God. He travels to dreaded Nineveh and announces God's imminent judgment. Incredibly, the Ninevites repent. What is perhaps less understandable is Jonah's reaction to his miraculous success in Nineveh. But here we learn the true reason why Jonah had initially refused to go. It was not because he was afraid that the Ninevites would reject his message and kill him. He was afraid that they might actually listen, repent, and be forgiven by God. He feared that God's forbearance and mercy might also extend to Israel's enemies.

> But this was very displeasing to Jonah, and he became angry. He prayed to the LORD and said, "O LORD! Is not this what I said while I was still in my own country? That is why I fled to Tarshish at the beginning; for I knew that you are a gracious God and merciful, slow to anger, and abounding in steadfast love, and ready to relent from punishing. And now, O LORD, please take my life from me, for it is better for me to die than to live." (4:1–3)

Hear God's response in verse 11:

> And should I not be concerned about Nineveh, that great city, in which there are more than a hundred and twenty thousand persons who do not know their right hand from their left, and also many animals?

What Jonah and the traditions of Ruth, Isaiah, and (likely) Malachi have in common is that they are urging their fellow Israelites to reclaim an element of their heritage and calling that is as ancient as their ancestor Abraham. When God calls Abram in Genesis 12:1–3, it is for the purpose of creating a people that will be God's own, a "treasured possession out of all the peoples" as God puts it in Exodus 19:5. Yet God's creation of this people from Abram was not simply for their own sake. Along with the gift of blessing, God also gives Abram and his descendants a calling: "and through you all the nations of the earth shall be blessed" (Gen 12:3). Thus the "treasured possession," by its trust in God and obedience to God's ways, was also to be a "Priestly Kingdom" and a "Holy Nation" (Exod 19:6). They were to be a people set apart as priests, those who call the nations to repentance, who instruct the nations in the ways of God, who celebrate the faithful role Gentiles have played in their history, and who rejoice when foreigners and eunuchs are gathered with them into God's household.

SOCIAL MOVEMENT AND COUNTERMOVEMENT

Recognizing the commonality of social movements and countermovements at pivotal periods of a society's history provides a useful framework for engaging these Israelite traditions. If we simply followed the canonical arrangement of these traditions, for instance, and didn't look for ways in which the traditions dated to this period might reflect different understandings among Israelites on how they are to live as the people of God at this crucial juncture of their history, we would likely overlook the scope and significance of the conflict they reflect, and our understanding of these texts would be the poorer for it.

To be sure, one of the compelling features of this conflict is that it reflects two groups of Israelites, at the same point in time, drawing from their sacred traditions in order to legitimate two completely different responses to the matter of Gentile inclusion. The one group looks back and focuses on those traditions that call Israel to remain separate from the peoples of the land. The other group looks back and instead believes that the time was now right to embrace those traditions with a more inclusive orientation, and take up their call to welcome and minister to the people of the land. And even more remarkably, these two very different perspectives on how to live as God's people at this point in time were then preserved by the framers of the Israelite canon and eventually authorized as sacred Scripture.

Moreover, the insights we gain from cultural anthropology also lead us to engage more fully—or at least ponder—the intertwining of religious, social, and political realities in these texts. On the surface, the argument among Israelites in the early Second Temple Period over whether or not Israelites can take non-Israelites as husbands and wives may seem to be primarily, if not exclusively, a religious one. But is that all this conflict is about? Of course not! Here are some additional issues this complex of texts in their settings raise that would be worth further exploration.

1. Those advocating for Israel's separation from surrounding peoples include those at the apex of Israel's elite. While many Israelite officials have taken for themselves Israelite wives, Ezra and Nehemiah, both of whom serve with the mandate of the Persian king, are at the forefront of this countermovement to maintain Israel's ethnic purity. The voices expressing a different perspective were prominent enough to gain a foothold and become codified in several Israelite traditions, but they seem to be on the margins of Israelite political power, at least within Jerusalem. Why is this so? Were there certain social, environmental, or

psychological factors that made the countermovement more politically viable at this point in Israel's history? Is it a common tendency among groups in the process of reconstituting themselves in the aftermath of tragedy and near dissolution to adopt a separatist orientation? What is the relationship between genealogical purity and social identity and stability?

2. The book of Ezra indicates that Ezra was joined in his passionate and public display of remorse over the intermingling of Israelites with non-Israelites by a "very great assembly of men, women, and children" (10:1). The remedy of divorce and deportation is also first suggested by Shecaniah, who cites the authority of God's Torah and describes the faithful as "those who tremble at the commandment of God" (v. 3). Additionally, the account does not indicate any substantial dissent. At a cursory glance, this action seems to be endorsed by nearly all of Israel. However, we are told immediately after Shecaniah's proposal that "Ezra stood up and made the leading priests, the Levites, and all Israel swear that they would do as had been said. And so they swear" (v. 5). The action is initiated with an authoritarian, even divine, mandate and compulsory oath-taking.

3. Relatedly, as already noted, those refusing to comply with the order to assemble in Jerusalem would face forfeiture of their landholdings and banishment from the restored exiles (v. 8). In short, political power and extreme economic and social pressure were mechanisms used to ensure compliance to the mandate for divorce and deportation. This invites us to assume that this mandate action was met with resistance by some, if not many, among the returned exiles. This also returns us to the question above, though it may be useful to ask it from a different angle: Was such exclusivism a natural development in light of the circumstances facing this Judean community, or was it imposed by the Jerusalem elite on the returned exiles despite the tendencies of many to loosen the boundaries between "Israel" and others?

4. Some scholars have suggested that the congregation of the returned exiles in Jerusalem became a somewhat distinct community that adopted an elevated self-understanding and identity vis-à-vis their fellow Israelites remaining in the diaspora. Did the separatist policies of Ezra and Nehemiah become characteristic of the returned exiles in Jerusalem, while an inclusive perspective prevailed among Israelites in the diaspora? Was the embrace of the exclusive perspective required to belong to the Jerusalem community?

5. As we saw, Israelite sacred tradition preserves both inclusive and exclusive streams of tradition, and at times intertwines them in very

interesting ways (e.g., Hagar). What is the relationship between the formation of the Israelite canon and this conflict over Gentiles within Israel? Does the presence of these two streams of tradition in the canon reflect Israel's attempt to negotiate a compromise between these variant perspectives at a time when Israel's sacred traditions were likely being redacted, codified, and gathered into collections?

CONCLUSION

The anthropological models of "social movement" and "countermovement" provide us with additional tools for understanding the biblical writings in relation to their social contexts. These models help us appreciate the many instances in which the biblical texts functioned as "resistance literature," countering the dominant norms of their wider societies or even their own communities. Moreover, they help us account for the diversity of perspectives we sometimes find embedded within the biblical traditions by calling us to recognize that human societies—even the most stable ones—inevitably give rise to deviation and change *and* subsequent attempts to restore or maintain established patterns. Care must be taken, however, to ensure that we utilize these models in ways that fit the particular features of any given moment in the lives of Israel and the early Christian community. Not only must the biblical texts be read in conversation with their particular social contexts, so too must the models we employ to help us better understand those contexts.

5.

Purity: Things in Their Proper Place

Luke relays this story of a "sinful" woman crashing a dinner party of Simon the Pharisee (7:36–50).

[36] One of the Pharisees asked Jesus to eat with him, and he went into the Pharisee's house and took his place at the table. [37] And a woman in the city, who was a sinner, having learned that he was eating in the Pharisee's house, brought an alabaster jar of ointment. [38] She stood behind him at his feet, weeping, and began to bathe his feet with her tears and to dry them with her hair. Then she continued kissing his feet and anointing them with the ointment. [39] Now when the Pharisee who had invited him saw it, he said to himself, "If this man were a prophet, he would have known who and what kind of woman this is who is touching him—that she is a sinner." [40] Jesus spoke up and said to him, "Simon, I have something to say to you." "Teacher," he replied, "speak." [41] "A certain creditor had two debtors; one owed five hundred denarii, and the other fifty. [42] When they could not pay, he canceled the debts for both of them. Now which of them will love him more?" [43] Simon answered, "I suppose the one for whom he canceled the greater debt." And Jesus said to him, "You have judged rightly." [44] Then turning towards the woman, he said to Simon, "Do you see this woman? I entered your house; you gave me no water for my feet, but she has bathed my feet with her tears and dried them with her hair. [45] You gave me no kiss, but from the time I came in she has not stopped kissing my feet. [46] You did not anoint my head with oil, but she has anointed my feet with ointment. [47] Therefore, I tell you, her sins, which were many, have been forgiven; hence she has shown great love. But the one to whom little is forgiven, loves little." [48] Then he said to her, "Your sins are forgiven." [49] But those who were at the table with him began to say among themselves, "Who is this who even forgives sins?" [50] And he said to the woman, "Your faith has saved you; go in peace."

Consider Luke's description of the scene. His repeated mention of "Pharisees" / "Pharisee's house" in the opening verses (vv. 36–37) reinforces the atmosphere of high decorum surrounding that space. Luke thus accentuates the scandalous nature of the uninvited guest's trespass, as "a woman in the city, who was a sinner" enters a domain forbidden to all like her (v. 37). Even more disturbing, this trespasser and transgressor of decency begins fawning over Jesus. Here the narrative slows, as Luke encourages the recipient to attend to each of the woman's acts of humble yet indecorous devotion: standing behind Jesus at his feet and weeping, she engages in the continuous activity (note the imperfect tense in Greek) of bathing his feet with her tears, drying them with her hair, kissing his feet, and anointing them with costly perfume (vv. 37–38). Although we do not know the reason why the woman is regarded as "sinful" by her community, the woman's very presence and even more so her intimate actions in the context of a dinner gathering would be seen by nearly all in this culture as "out of place." The woman's devotion may also be seen as having an erotic edge, adding to the scandalous nature of her trespass. No wonder Simon the Pharisee is beside himself and doubts Jesus's prophetic insight: "If this man were a prophet, he would have known who and what kind of woman this is who is touching him—that she is a sinner!" (v. 39).

Beyond the social transgressions embodied in the sinful woman's presence and actions, several features of Luke's account suggest that purity concerns are also in view. The setting of Simon's home, with guests at table, establishes an atmosphere not only of high decorum and social prestige but one in which purity is closely guarded. The Pharisaic attention to purity was likely well known to Luke's audience, and the surrounding narrative also establishes purity as one of the Pharisees' central concerns (5:27–32; 6:1–11; 11:37–40). Meal settings were not only attentive to the honor and social location of those involved, but scrupulous Israelites in Jesus's day refused to share table with Gentiles and other sinners due to the danger of "cross-contamination." Note too Simon's disgust that a woman such as this is *touching* Jesus. His words signal the emphasis Luke places on the woman's physical interaction with Jesus, evident from the clear parallels between its initial description by Luke and then Jesus's commendation of the woman's devotion:

> She stood behind him at his feet, weeping, and began to bathe his feet with her tears and to dry them with her hair. Then she continued kissing his feet and anointing them with the ointment. (v. 38)

> Then turning towards the woman, he said to Simon, "Do you see this woman? I entered your house; you gave me no water for my feet, but she has bathed my feet with her tears and dried them with her hair. You gave me no kiss, but from the time I came in she has not stopped kissing my feet. You did not anoint my head with oil, but she has anointed my feet with ointment." (vv. 44–46)

Thus, Luke's casting of the setting and its characters suggests that this woman of ill-repute—at least from the perspective of Simon and his other guests (and perhaps many of Luke's recipients!)—"comes into this scene like an alien, communicable disease."[1] She is a dirty woman. Worse still, she radiates dirt. But how does this perception of her character by Simon and his comrades—and Jesus's regard for their perspective as a tragic *misperception*—contribute to the rhetorical edge and energy of Luke's account? Isn't it enough simply to realize that this here is a woman of ill-repute at the bottom of the social spectrum who acts in ways that flagrantly transgress social custom, while Simon and his table-mates are respected persons who act to protect the social boundaries guarding his house? Why, in other words, does her *impurity* matter?

PURITY IN JESUS'S CONTEXT:
THREE UNRESOLVED QUESTIONS

Many modern readers of Scripture, especially those within the Christian tradition, tend to associate purity concerns of ancient Israelites almost exclusively with the avoidance of certain physical substances or foods. This, I think, contributes to a second tendency among such readers: to regard the purity matters addressed or assumed in the Bible as peculiarities of a bygone era which are fortunately irrelevant for us today. For such readers, purity is a marginal, easily overlooked dimension of the biblical tradition.

Among scholars, however, purity has become a subject of much discussion and debate, while proving to be a complex and unwieldy topic. This has been especially the case with respect to the following questions emerging from the realm of NT studies: (1) the prevalence and type of purity practices among Israelite folk in the two centuries straddling the start of the Common Era (100 BCE–100 CE); (2) the role of the Pharisees in promoting purity practices in the first century CE; and (3) Jesus's response to the Pharisees and their conceptions of purity as portrayed by the gospels. Scholars have sometimes turned to the insights and

1. Joel B. Green, *The Gospel of Luke*, NICNT (Grand Rapids: Eerdmans, 1997), 307.

resources of cultural anthropology, and anthropology in general, to help them make sense of these challenging matters. We will use the following pages to explore some of their research and reflection. The previous chapters have each introduced and illustrated several insights that cultural anthropology has contributed to the study of the biblical traditions in general. This chapter will take a slightly different tack. It will continue to illustrate the potential benefits cultural anthropology offers to biblical interpretation, but here by focusing in on the tricky reality of purity, and these particular questions scholars have struggled to answer.

CONTRIBUTIONS OF CULTURAL ANTHROPOLOGY TO OUR UNDERSTANDING OF PURITY

Prior to zeroing in on these three pernicious questions related to purity emerging from the study of the NT texts, it will be necessary for us to review the ways that cultural anthropology has shaped the study and perception of purity in general, and Israelite purity in particular. In this section I will identify and discuss four broader contributions cultural anthropology has made to our understanding of purity that are relevant to the exploration of these three questions.

1. Cultural anthropology provides a paradigm for understanding what purity is essentially about: symbolic enactments of an underlying system of order and purpose.

Purity and impurity, clean and unclean, is about dirty things and dirty people. But anthropologists have helped us to understand that purity concepts and practices are also about much more than dirt. Numerous anthropologists have contributed to this discussion, but chief among them is Mary Douglas, whose text *Purity and Danger* is regarded by many still today as an important touchstone for the study of purity.[2] Douglas's main contributions to our understanding of purity consist of the following:[3]

    a. Purity represents normality and wholeness—the way things should be.

    b. Determinations of purity result not from objective physical reality but from the cultural understandings of a particular community.[4]

---

2. Mary Douglas, *Purity and Danger: An Analysis of the Concepts of Pollution and Taboo* (London: Routledge & Kegan Paul, 1966, 2002).

3. This list is adapted from David Wright, "Unclean and Clean (OT)," *ABD* 6 (1992): 739.

4. Similarly, scholars of purity systems point out that purity in ancient contexts is not neces-

They are socially inscribed and are held in variant forms by different cultures.

c. Purity rules are symbols that express and reflect a broad array of social concerns. In a society with a highly developed purity system, these rules can also reflect its cosmology and understanding of the social order as a whole, including its members' proper relationships with the divine, creation, one another, and other humans. The cultural distinction of "clean" and "unclean" "orders the complexity of reality by defining and imposing upon it internal as well as external boundaries."[5] In other words, as Douglas explains,

> Where there is dirt, there is a system. Dirt is the product of a systemic ordering and classification of matter, in so far as ordering involves rejecting inappropriate elements. This idea of dirt takes us straight into the field of symbolism and promises a link-up with more obviously symbolic systems of purity.[6]

Or, as Douglas states in a later work,

> The idea of dirt implies a structure of idea. For us dirt is a kind of compendium category for all events which blur, smudge, contradict, or otherwise confuse accepted classifications. The underlying feeling is that a system of values which is habitually expressed in a given arrangement of things has been violated.[7]

d. The body is a symbol for or a microcosm of the larger social body. Thus, the body is a locus where purity concerns are manifested. Concerns about things entering and exiting the body reflect concerns about the boundaries of society.

Some elements of Douglas's theory on purity have come under criticism. Most notably, several scholars have questioned the extent to which all purity rules of a given society have a clear symbolic function. Some purity codes may have become part of a culture in a more ad hoc fashion due to outside influences, or a group's interaction with its physical environment, or the idiosyncratic tendencies of certain leaders. And "even

sarily, if at all, connected to hygiene or food safety. Ancient persons simply did not share our understanding of bacterial or viral transmission or infection.

5. Christian Frevel and Christophe Nihan, "Introduction," in *Purity and the Forming of Religious Traditions in the Ancient Mediterranean World and Ancient Judaism*, ed. Christian Frevel and Christophe Nihan (Leiden: Brill, 2013), 5.

6. Douglas, *Purity and Danger* (2002), 44.

7. Mary Douglas, *Implicit Meanings: Mary Douglas: Collected Works* (New York: Routledge, 1975, 2003), 109.

if we grant that pollution beliefs are somehow connected, at a very general level, with the delineation of boundaries in a given culture or social group, this does not automatically imply that all pollution beliefs may legitimately be viewed as cultural or religious symbols."[8] Relatedly, Douglas's model assumes that purity rules develop in societies in order to express and validate already-existing divisions within a social group. Others, however, have argued that the relationship between social boundaries and the complex systems that evolve to frame and legitimate them is likely more dialectical and dynamic than *Purity and Danger* appreciates. Finally, when Douglas applies her pollution theory to the biblical texts, many find that she tries too hard to force several elements of Old Testament cosmology, especially divisions between clean and unclean animals, into clear patterns of internal and external boundaries. In so doing, she initially advocates several somewhat tortured readings of Old Testament traditions.[9]

Despite the merit of these criticisms, Douglas's insight that purity rules and rituals—to some notable degree—give symbolic expression to a society's shared conceptions of the world and people's proper relations to the divine, one another, and the rest of the cosmos, remains the standard approach to the study of purity customs in many cultures, including the cultures that shaped the biblical writings. It is not an exaggeration to say that for most scholars seeking to utilize anthropological models to better understand the biblical conceptions of clean and unclean, her work has been determinative. Before we go on to discuss two additional contributions cultural anthropology has made to the study of purity in the biblical writings, we will pause here to overview the manifestation of purity within the Israelite Scriptures as described by scholars who are indebted to Douglas's approach.

THE ESSENTIALS OF ISRAELITE PURITY

Central to Douglas's conception of purity is the notion that everything has a place. Purity occurs when things are in their proper place. Impurity results when they are not. Here is a crude example that I hope will provide an efficient illustration of this concept without "grossing out" too

---

8. Frevel and Nihan, "Introduction," *Purity*, ed. Frevel and Nihan, 7.

9. Douglas herself laments what she later came to see as her misreading of these traditions. In the preface to the 2002 Routledge Classics edition of her work (p. xvi), she retracts some of these readings with the humble (and commendable) acknowledgment: "I was way out of my depth when I wrote Chapter 3 of this book nearly forty years ago. I made mistakes about the Bible for which I have been very sorry ever since. Longevity is a blessing in that it gave me time to discover them."

many of you: toe- or fingernails are in their proper place when they are attached to a toe or finger. In fact, many in our culture invest time and resources to maintain and even beautify these very useful appendage coverings. But for most people in our culture, nail clippings are out of place when they appear under bedcovers, on the kitchen table, or between someone's teeth. At that point, what are otherwise beneficial and even celebrated parts of us become *unclean*.

Mapping Creation

Yet as Douglas helps us to see, within the Israelite Scriptures, as in numerous other cultures, purity involves more than just clean and unclean people or things. As Douglas emphasized, clean and unclean things are designated as such because of an underlying system that manifests a particular worldview: namely, they have a symbolic function. The symbolic function of many Israelite purity laws radiates out from the creation story of Genesis 1. This "cosmogonic myth"—a story of the origins of the cosmos that expresses fundamental elements of a tradition's worldview—articulates the essentials of Israelite cosmology and how things are to be ordered in creation. This cosmology "encoded various 'maps' or configurations of lines which God made for Israel to perceive and follow."[10] These maps "order, classify, and define the world" as Israelites came to see it.[11] During creation, God established a map of *time*, the separation of day and night, the seven-day week, with the last being a day of rest, with celestial bodies to regulate its passing. A map of *things* identified features of the physical and animal world, with animals being separated in terms of their proper place, sources of nourishment, and types of movement. A map of *place* separated dry land from the waters, the heavens above from the earth below, and the realms where God's creatures are to dwell. A map of *diet* was assigned each creature according to its kind. And a map of *status* was unveiled as the hierarchy of creation was established: the heavens rule over the night, the sun over the day, and humans over the animals of creation. Thus, the creation story of Genesis 1 establishes the basic template for what emerged as the Israelite sense of normalcy as ordained by God. This is the divine order of things essential to the world of blessing, life, and wholeness that God has called

10. Jerome Neyrey, "The Symbolic Universe of Luke–Acts: 'They Turn the World Upside Down,'" in *The Social World of Luke–Acts: Models for Interpretation*, ed. Jerome Neyrey (Peabody, MA: Hendrickson, 1991), 277. The identification and descriptions of the various maps to follow are adapted from Neyrey's chapter.

11. Neyrey, "Symbolic Universe of Luke–Acts," 277.

into being. To put it most simply, everything has a place. Purity is about where the stuff of life belongs so that creation can function as it should.

Mapping Israelite Society

There is, of course, a lot of "stuff" to life. And the Israelite Torah developed, in part, as an account of where the stuff of life was to be placed and how it was to be ordered. In concert with the patterning suggested in Genesis 1, the Israelite sense of clean and unclean revolved around one of the core elements of their worldview: God's *holiness*. I think it is common for people today to associate holiness with "cleanliness." But that association is secondary to the basic meanings of the term. God's holiness was understood as God's unmatched ability to bless and to curse, to order creation in a manner consistent with God's character and will. This is why numerous Israelite traditions associate God's holiness with God's sovereignty over creation *and* celebrate such holiness alongside God's gracious provision and mercy. To take just one example among many, in Psalm 86, a lament seeking deliverance from enemies, the psalmist celebrates God's unique, holy sovereignty that executes blessing as one of the reasons why God should again act to preserve life (vv. 8–10):

> There is none like you among the gods, O Lord,
>   nor are there any works like yours.
> All the nations you have made shall come
>   and bow down before you, O Lord,
>   and shall glorify your name.
> For you are great and do wondrous things;
>   you alone are God.

But from an Israelite perspective, holiness was not to be characteristic of God alone: "You shall be holy, for I the Lord your God am holy" (Lev 19:2). Israel itself, as God's people, was to be a holy people:

> At the third new moon after the Israelites had gone out of the land of Egypt, on that very day, they came into the wilderness of Sinai. They had journeyed from Rephidim, entered the wilderness of Sinai, and camped in the wilderness; Israel camped there in front of the mountain. Then Moses went up to God; the Lord called to him from the mountain, saying, "Thus you shall say to the house of Jacob, and tell the Israelites: You have seen what I did to the Egyptians, and how I bore you on eagles' wings and brought you to myself. Now therefore, if you obey my voice and keep my covenant, you shall be my treasured possession out of all the peoples. Indeed, the whole

earth is mine, but you shall be for me a priestly kingdom and a holy nation. These are the words that you shall speak to the Israelites." (Exod 19:1–6)

It is from Israel's calling to be a special recipient and agent of God's blessing (starting with Abram back in Gen 12:1–3) that the idea of Israel being "set apart" by God derives. And as a people set apart by God to be recipients and agents of blessing, to be a *holy* nation, Israel is to order its common life in ways that set itself apart from others and that enable Israel to live in a blessed relationship with its holy God, one another, and the rest of creation. It is for this reason that Israel must be pure, or clean, or *do things properly*. Purity is a consequence of Israel's vocation as God's holy people. Actually, that fails to state the matter strongly enough. It is on a proper ordering of life—or proper relationships with God and other persons and things—that Israel's vocation as God's holy people *wholly* depends. For this reason, God's gift of Torah follows (in Exodus 20) the vocational mandate God grants Israel (Exodus 19).

Because the preceding paragraphs have just trotted out a flurry of connecting ideas in a rather short span of space, here is a brief review of how these concepts fit together:

- God is holy.

- This means that God has unmatched power to bless, to order creation for life.

- Israel is called to be holy as God is holy: a holy nation of a holy God.

- As a people set apart as recipients and agents of blessing, Israel is to order its life in ways that distinguish Israel from others, facilitate its intimate relationship with God, and enable it to fulfill its vocation.

So how was Israel to order its life in ways that facilitated its identity as recipients and agents of God's blessing? Here the insights of Douglas also prove helpful. The logic reflected in Israel's "way of life" was the logic Israel discerned from God's act of ordering a creation in which everything had a place, and to have a place was to be blessed.[12] To be holy as God was holy meant that Israel was to order its communal life, its worship life (which eventually centered around the temple), and even creation itself, in ways Israel discerned were consistent with God's ordering

---

12. Note that God's life-giving blessing and command to be fruitful and multiply is given to both humans *and* the other creatures of creation (Gen 1:22, 28).

of creation and God's will for them. Therefore, the mapping of creation in Genesis 1 is paralleled by the mapping of Israelite society we find reflected in Israel's ancient traditions, especially in the Torah. Rooted in these Torah traditions, Israelites in Jesus's day mapped their world in ways that still reflected their understanding of God as Holy, Sovereign Creator, and their identity as God's holy people. Note the clear parallels in what follows to the mapping provided by Genesis 1 we identified above:

> There were maps of (1) *time*, which specified rules for the sabbath, when to say the *Shema*, and when circumcision should be performed; (2) *places*, spelling out what could be done in the various precincts of the Temple or where the scapegoat was to be sent on the Day of Atonement; (3) *persons*, designating whom one could marry, touch, or eat with; who could divorce; who could enter the various spaces in the Temple and Temple courtyards; and who could hold certain offices or perform certain actions; (4) *things*, clarifying what was considered clean or unclean, could be offered in sacrifice, or could be allowed contact with the body; (5) *meals*, determining what could be eaten; how it was to be grown, prepared, or slaughtered; in what vessels it could be served; when and where it could be eaten; and with whom it could be shared; and (6) "*others*," that is, whoever and whatever could pollute by contact.[13]

Later in this chapter, we will have the opportunity to fill out the general contours of this map with some additional specifics. Now we need to resume our conversation about the four broad contributions cultural anthropology has made to our understanding of purity in general and Israelite purity in particular. But before we do, here are two caveats that will be useful to keep in mind as the rest of the chapter unfolds. First, at this stage of the discussion I have focused on the lines of continuity that exist between the mapping of Israelite society in place in the first century CE with the mapping of creation suggested in Genesis 1. I have done this to illustrate and emphasize the symbolic function of Israel's purity system, and its enactment of fundamental elements of Israel's worldview. But this does not mean (and here again is where Douglas's initial analysis struggled) that one can rightly draw clear lines of connection from every specific purity rule to the mapping of creation in Genesis 1. There simply does not seem to be that degree of alignment, and attempts to find such clear parallels with every purity-related code result in forced readings of Israel's legal traditions. Some purity laws are more clearly connected to the map of Genesis 1 than others. While the model Douglas proposed works very well in a general sense, it does not account for every purity tradition at any stage of Israel's history.

Second, numerous scholars offering close readings of purity codes in Israel's Scriptures have pointed out some degree of variation within those traditions, including traditions as closely related as Leviticus, Deuteronomy, and Numbers.[14] We also saw in chapter 4 significant diversity reflected in early Second Temple traditions over the matter of marriage between Israelites and Gentiles (or "genealogical purity"). Israelite tradition prior to the first century CE does not provide a univocal witness of how the map of Genesis 1 is to be mapped out in Israelite society. Above, I recorded Douglas's observation that purity codes are socially inscribed and are held in variant forms by different cultures. But we also find such variation *within* cultures. As could be expected, purity practices and their symbolic reference fluctuate and evolve over time and can also be practiced differently by Israelites at the same time. So, as we attempt to understand Israelite purity, we will likely be less frustrated if we keep in mind that Israelite purity practices and concepts can in some ways be doggone untidy.

2. Cross-cultural analysis enables us to draw comparisons between Israelite purity codes and other traditions of the ancient Mediterranean.

In a volume titled *Purity and the Forming of Religious Traditions in the Ancient Mediterranean World and Ancient Judaism*, several scholars report on conceptions and practices of purity in various cultures of the Ancient Mediterranean, including Mesopotamian, Egyptian, Anatolian, Phoenician, Grecian, Zoroastrian, Roman, and Israelite. In their introduction to the volume, the editors Christian Frevel and Christophe Nihan detail several common features of purity practice among these ancient Mediterranean cultures. Their observations fall roughly into two categories. First, Frevel and Nihan observe that one basic feature emerging in several of the studies contained in the volume is that purity concepts and practices constitute "a central aspect of the implementation of social practice in a given group."[15] In other words, purity concepts and rituals are integral to the social life and character of each of these cultures. Second, the cross-cultural analysis provided by the studies in the volume

---

14. See, for example, Christophe Nihan, "Forms and Functions of Purity in Leviticus," in *Purity and the Forming of Religious Traditions in the Ancient Mediterranean World and Ancient Judaism*, ed. Christian Frevel and Christophe Nihan (Leiden: Brill, 2013); Frevel, "Purity Conceptions in the Book of Numbers in Context," in *Purity*, ed. Frevel and Nihan; Udo Rütersworden, "Purity Conceptions in Deuteronomy," in Frevel and Nihan, *Purity*.

15. Frevel and Nihan, *Purity*, 36.

also lead Frevel and Nihan to conclude that purity also plays a critical role in the formation and transformation of religious traditions. I list and briefly describe these observations here and will draw from them later in our discussion of Israelite purity practices and the role of the Pharisees in the first century CE.

PURITY AND THE CONSTRUCTION OF SOCIAL PRACTICE

Frevel and Nihan argue that the concepts of purity and impurity "[correspond] first and foremost to the collective ascription, within a group, of a distinct status, which is itself related to a series of social roles."[16] Moreover, impurity is often, if not always, a category of social exclusion that calls for the performance of socially codified practices in order to return to a state defined as "clean." While the specific features of purity concepts and practices vary from one Mediterranean culture to another, Frevel and Nihan discern the following commonalities:

a. Purity concepts are grounded in and mirror a society's understanding of its relationship with its deities: "the opposition between pure and impure serves first and foremost to define a key aspect of the relationship between human beings (male and female) and deities, which can then be used, so to speak, in a derivative manner, in order to construe and conceptualize the relationships between in-group and out-group, or within the group itself."[17]

b. The opposition between pure and impure is (as we saw above) related to the social construction of space, especially the division between sacred and profane space. Consequently, purity codes define and restrict access to gods and sanctuaries, and even to households. Therefore, the mapping of sacred space defines who is permitted to participate in local cults and their rituals. Furthermore, this function of purity is "a central aspect of the definition of collective and personal identity and agency."[18]

c. Finally, in these cultures purity also defines a select group of "ritual specialists" qualified to distinguish between pure and impure and enact the rituals that can return persons to purity. As a result, the purity systems of these cultures enact the empowerment of priestly authority.

16. Frevel and Nihan, *Purity*, 36.
17. Frevel and Nihan, *Purity*, 37.
18. Frevel and Nihan, *Purity*, 38.

PURITY AND THE FORMATION AND TRANSFORMATION
OF RELIGIOUS TRADITIONS

Frevel and Nihan find that conceptions and practices of purity are remarkably persistent but also adaptable during critical moments of development and transformation within religious traditions. The opposition between purity and impurity endures, but the precise contours of that opposition morph as a central component of a culture's religious transformation. More specifically:

a. Purity norms are remarkably stable throughout much of ancient Mediterranean history, but major changes in conceptions often reflect significant social, economic, political, cultural, or cultic transformations. Consequently, the development and transformation of purity concepts prove to function as an excellent indicator of broader cultural changes and their impact on religious traditions.

b. Significant adjustments in purity practices throughout the Mediterranean region during the first millennium BCE resulted not only as a reaction to Hellenism but also from a broad yet complex array of cultural, religious, and economic factors beginning with Persian rule. One implication of this finding is that the emphasis on purity in Hellenistic Judaism is not an isolated phenomenon but needs to be addressed against the background of a more general cultural development taking place throughout the ancient Mediterranean.

c. In contexts of dispute during the latter half of the first millennium BCE, purity concepts emerge as attempts to stigmatize various categories of practice and persons, especially within Judaism.[19] This stigmatization is aimed at both internal and external differentiation, and likely results from significant disagreements among Israelites on the defining markers of Judaism. Moreover, there is also a tendency within Mediterranean traditions during this time, and again especially within Judaism, to merge together what had been distinct forms of purity (such as ritual/physical and moral purity). To these more generalized concepts of purity are then added new conceptions of pollution as an attempt to stigmatize others and further differentiate one's group from them.

d. Also, during the latter half of the first millennium BCE (and earlier for some groups), one key cultural shift in the formation and devel-

19. Frevel and Nihan, *Purity*, 41–42. Here Frevel and Nihan are drawing from Benedikt Rausche, "The Relevance of Purity in Second Temple Judaism according to Ezra–Nehemiah," in *Purity*, ed. Frevel and Nihan, 457–76, and Beate Ego, "Purity Concepts in Jewish Traditions of the Hellenistic Period," in *Purity*, ed. Frevel and Nihan, 477–92.

opment of a religious tradition is reference to a body of texts that functions as a central authority. This "textualization" of key religious traditions often leads to their sacralization by the group, conferring on them a sacred status. This tends to reinforce and invigorate the practice of purity for a wider array of persons within these traditions, since the texts valuing and defining purity practices are no longer confined to a sacred space or to local customs. In short, they become accessible to a wider array of people, who then tend to view those purity practices as relevant to their own contexts and practices.

3. Archaeology has made significant contributions to our understanding of Israelite purity practices in the late Second Temple Period.

Numerous textual sources from the late Second Temple Period (first century BCE until 70 CE) indicate a concern with the ritual purity laws found in the Torah, especially those sections contained in the Priestly Code (mostly in Leviticus 11–15 and Numbers 19). These laws detail numerous sources of ritual impurity, such as male and female genital discharges, various skin diseases, as well as human and certain animal corpses. The biblical apocrypha and pseudepigrapha, the Dead Sea Scrolls, the New Testament, and the works of Philo and Flavius Josephus include numerous references to these laws and the ways they were implemented by various Jewish groups.[20]

Recent archaeological discoveries over the last three decades have given us a fuller picture of the contours and extent of these purity practices among Israelites during this period. Archaeologists have found an increasing number of ritual baths (*mikva'ot*) and various stone jars, cups, and bowls throughout areas of Palestine inhabited by Israelites from about 150 BCE to 135 CE. Stone vessels are widespread throughout the region. *Mikva'ot*, while concentrated in and around Jerusalem, have also been located in outlying towns and villages, including in Galilee and at Qumran. As reported by Yonatan Adler,

> Ritual baths from this period have been discovered at dozens of sites throughout Israel, from the Upper Galilee and the Golan in the north, to the Beersheba valley in the south, as well as at a number of sites in Jordan. Not surprisingly, the largest concentration of ritual baths dating to the Early Roman period has been found in Jerusalem, where approximately 170 baths have been uncovered to date. The phenomenon is hardly one unique to Jerusalem, however, as hundreds of ritual baths dating to the Early Roman

20. Yonatan Adler, "Jewish Purity Practices in Roman Judea: The Evidence of Archaeology," ASOR Blog, February 2017, https://tinyurl.com/y78xd6c.

period have been uncovered at dozens of rural settlement sites in the Judean countryside. Often numerous baths have been found at a single site, even in relatively small villages or farmsteads, a phenomenon which highlights the important role that ritual immersion played in the daily lives of Jews during this period.[21]

According to later Rabbinic texts, stone vessels were impervious to impurity, and in light of the preponderance of these vessels this view seems likely among many Israelites in the first century CE.[22] As a result, these vessels would have protected bearers of impure liquids from contamination, as well as clean foods and liquids from contamination outside those vessels. This feature would have also allowed the continued use of vessels that had once held unclean substances. According to the Rabbis, fired clay, leather, bone, glass, and wooden vessels were to be destroyed once contaminated by unclean substances.[23] Also from Rabbinic and Qumran texts we learn that stepped pools were used for the washing or immersion of persons, clothing, and other objects to cleanse from impurity, or to shorten the period during which one would be considered unclean.

While it can be precarious to read practices attested in later Rabbinic tradition back into the first century CE, these Rabbinic traditions, along with other textual witnesses from the New Testament and the DSS texts to similar purity concerns, strongly suggest that the preponderance of stone vessels and *mikva'ot* reflect rather widespread purity practices among Israelites in the land of Israel across the social spectrum.[24] To be sure, scholars have debated the identification of the *mikva'ot*, and the criteria for distinguishing them from cisterns or regular bathing facilities. Some have argued that the preponderance of stone vessels may be due

21. Adler, "Jewish Purity Practices." In this 2017 blog post Adler provides a concise overview of these archaeological findings and their relevance. For a more detailed review, see Yonatan Adler, "Between Priestly Cult and Common Culture: The Material Evidence of Ritual Purity Observance in Early Roman Jerusalem Reassessed," *Journal of Ancient Judaism* 7 (2016): 228–48; Stuart Miller, *At the Intersection of Texts and Material Finds: Stepped Pools, Stone Vessels and Ritual Purity among the Jews of Roman Galilee*, JAJSup 16 (Göttingen: Vandenhoeck & Ruprecht, 2015), 307–32; Eyal Regev, "Non-Priestly Purity and Its Religious Aspects according to Historical Sources and Archaeological Findings," in *Purity and Holiness: The Heritage of Leviticus*, ed. M. J. H. M. Poorthuis and J. Schwartz (Leiden, Brill, 2000), 223–46; Jürgen Zangenberg, "Pure Stone: Archaeological Evidence for Jewish Purity Practices in Late Second Temple Judaism (Miqwa'ot and Stone Vessels)," in Frevel and Nihan, *Purity*, 537–72.

22. Although, as Jodi Magness reports in *Stone and Dung, Oil and Spit: Jewish Daily Life in the Time of Jesus* (Grand Rapids: Eerdmans, 2011), 75–76, Qumran literature states that stone and unfired earth and clay vessels become impure when contacted with oil.

23. Magness, *Stone and Dung*, 72–73.

24. Adler puts the current number of first-century *mikva'ot* unearthed in Palestine at about seven hundred.

to economic and technological developments more so than expanding purity practices among late Second Temple Israelites. But as the number of digs unearthing what appear to be ritual baths and stone vessels continue to mount, an increasing number of scholars believe that these artifacts, along with related textual traditions, create a compelling case that practices of "non-priestly purity" greatly expanded among Israelites in Palestine during the first century CE. As summarized by Thomas Kazen,

> During the Second Temple period, legal discussions were not as advanced, and halakhic development was not as detailed as in the *Mishnah, Tosephta* or *Talmudim*. But later materials can sometimes reflect early customs, and with the help of contemporary texts and archaeological evidence, a fairly balanced picture of the legal situation during the first century C.E. emerges. That is a picture of wide-spread concern for purity, although interpretations and degrees of consistency vary. I do not believe that immersion, purification of the hands, attentiveness in matters of liquids and handling of food, were concerns of a few *haberim* [groups especially attentive to matters of purity] only. Such customs were part of a fairly influential expansionist current in Second Temple Judaism.[25]

At the same time, just as Israelite tradition prior to the first century CE does not provide a univocal witness to how the map of Genesis 1 is to be mapped out in Israelite society, so too does there appear to be diverse understandings among Israelites at the turn of the Common Era on how stone vessels and stepped pools were to be properly utilized. This is indicated by the variability we find between Qumran and Rabbinic traditions, within Rabbinic traditions, and among the stepped pools themselves. As Stuart S. Miller stresses, "The ritual bathing *and other* purity practices of the rabbis evolved out of a complex matrix of practices that were derived from diverse understandings of the biblical tradition that existed during the pre-70 CE period."[26] As a result, "we err, therefore, in demanding or expecting a uniform understanding of ritual baths and continuity between ritual purity practices during the late Second Temple period and in the centuries following 70 CE."[27] Miller's point is made all the more cogent by another observation. So far we have been addressing purity practices among only a subset of Jewish folk in the late Second Temple Period: Israelites living in the homeland of Israel. Apart from a couple of Jewish intertestamental texts that may have originated in the Diaspora that mention handwashing before prayer—Pseudo

---

25. Thomas Kazen, *Jesus and Purity Halakhah: Was Jesus Indifferent to Impurity?* CB 38 (Winona Lake, IN: Eisenbrauns, 2010), 87.

26. Miller, *Texts and Material Finds*, 95.

27. Miller, *Texts and Material Finds*, 323.

Aristeas (305–6) and the *Third Sibylline Oracle* (3.591–93)—we simply do not find a similar concern for the purity practices of ritual immersion and the use of stone vessels reflected in the archaeological data among Jews in the diaspora.[28]

4. Great and Little Tradition

In chapter 3, I introduced the concept of Great Tradition and Little Tradition in our discussion of elite mastery over many elements of society. This is another resource from cultural anthropology that helps us to expect and account for diverse purity practices among Israelites during the late Second Temple Period and beyond. Allow me to fill out this concept more thoroughly here. The concepts of "Great" and "Little" Traditions were developed by cultural anthropologists in the 1950s. As anthropologist Milton Singer defines it, a Great Tradition is usually characterized as "a *learned* and *literate* tradition, preserving and developing the dominant systems of thought and value of a civilization."[29] Great Traditions are developed and championed by the ruling elite situated in urban areas, and are thus much more likely to be codified in literary documents. In contrast, Little Traditions are popular, rural, associated with villages, and are typically preserved in oral tradition.[30] As a result, their specific contours can be much more difficult to recover. While Great Traditions tend to preserve ancient ideals and practices, and thus often have a conservative dimension to them, they can also modify previous tradition in ways that benefit the ruling class. As a result, advocates of the Great Tradition may disparage proponents of Little Traditions that they view as outdated and simple-minded by comparison.[31] Here again we see the inextricable connection that often exists between social class, economics, and religious doctrine. And this particular feature of Great and Little Traditions will inform our assessment to follow of the purity dynamics manifested in Second Temple Judaism and in the NT.

INSIGHTS FROM CULTURAL ANTHROPOLOGY AND THE PROBLEM OF PURITY

Now that we have reviewed these four contributions cultural anthropology has made to our understanding of purity in general and Israelite

---

28. Magness, *Stone and Dung*, 186.

29. Milton Singer, *When a Great Tradition Modernizes: An Anthropological Approach to Indian Civilization* (New York: Praeger, 1972), 55.

30. Kazen, *Jesus and Purity*, 273.

31. See Malina, *New Testament World*, 87–88.

purity practices in particular, let us now return our attention to the issues related to the three purity and New Testament studies we identified above that have been particularly challenging for scholars: (1) the prevalence and type of purity practices among Israelite folk in the two centuries straddling the start of the Common Era (100 BCE–100 CE); (2) the role of the Pharisees in promoting purity practices in the first century CE; and (3) Jesus's response to the Pharisees and their conceptions of purity as portrayed by the gospels. Here I will suggest how the several anthropological insights we have just reviewed might contribute to our reflection on these contested matters.

PURITY PRACTICES AMONG ISRAELITE FOLK AT THE TURN OF THE COMMON ERA (100 BCE–100 CE)

The preceding discussion has helped us see that Israelite purity conceptions and practices, as was the case for other Mediterranean cultures, were integrally connected to their understanding of divine reality, creation, and their place in it. These practices "mapped out" proper ways of living in relationship to God, other persons, and the rest of creation. For Israelites during this period, maps of time circumscribed the observance of Sabbath, many other festivals, and rites of passage. Legal traditions developed various rules on what should and should not be done on the Sabbath. Maps of place defined sacred space and stipulated how it was to be engaged and protected. The symbolic center of sacred space for many Israelites was the temple. The temple itself was "mapped out," with its epicenter, the Holy of Holies, serving as the essential point of orientation from which all degrees of ritual purity were defined.

> In this arrangement, the Holy of Holies marks the center of the Temple Mount, which marks the center of Jerusalem, which marks the center of the holy land, which marks the center of the world. At the center of centers, God's holy people have the opportunity to interact with God under the ritual direction of God's priests aided by their Levites.[32]

The sacred space of temple also facilitated many Israelites' maps of people. As Malina stated above, the priests and their Levites facilitate Israel's interaction with God. Accordingly, the priests are atop the purity scale, followed by Levites and pureblooded Israelites.[33] These alone are the

---

32. Malina, *New Testament World*, 184–85.

33. I am indebted to Malina (*New Testament World*, 174–75) and Neyrey ("Symbolic Universe of Luke–Acts," 279) for the map of persons that follows. This map is, however, informed by Rabbinic sources.

ones that would have been considered "True Israel" by many Israelites, especially those promoting the Great Tradition.[34] A somewhat marginal set included bastard children of priests and proselyte converts. They were regarded as part of Israel. They could worship at the temple and could marry Levites and full-blooded Israelites but not priests. More marginal were bastards of nonpriestly Israelites, the fatherless, foundlings, and eunuchs. Members of these groups could worship at the temple, inter-marry, and marry converts, but they were forbidden to marry priests, Levites, full Israelites, and the illegal children of priests. More marginal still were eunuchs from birth and those with deformed sexual features. So marginal as to be off the purity scale of many Israelites were Gen-tiles—persons of all other ethnic groups. While conceptions of Gentile impurity varied among Israelites, many Jews avoided social contact with Gentiles, many prohibited intermarriage with Gentiles, and some regarded any physical contact with Gentiles a source of defilement.[35]

Maps of things and foods clarified what physical objects were con-sidered clean or unclean, could be offered in sacrifice, could be allowed contact with the body, or could be ingested. While this category also fluctuated among Israelites, the following substances are established in the Torah as being impure and were consistently held as such by most Jews of this period, corpses of animals and persons; seminal discharges, menstrual blood, and scale disease (commonly labeled as "leprosy"). As Jacob Milgrom observes:

> Their common denominator is death or the appearance of death. Vaginal blood and semen represent the forces of life. Their loss implies death. In the case of scale disease, its symbolism is made explicit by Aaron's prayer for Miriam, his stricken sister, "let her not be like a corpse" (Num 12:12).[36]

In light of the attention given to Jewish observance of dietary restrictions

34. Malina, *New Testament World*, 175.

35. Christine Hayes, in *Gentile Impurities and Jewish Identities: Intermarriage and Conversion from the Bible to the Talmud* (Oxford: Oxford University Press, 2002), 193–98, argues that many Israelites would have considered Gentiles *morally* and *genealogically* impure, but not necessar-ily *ritually* impure. According to Hayes among others, most Jews did not consider moral and genealogical impurity transmittable via touching, and so saw casual, social interaction with Gentiles as not defiling. Eating in the home of a Gentile was likely problematic due to the food that would be served, but other common transactions and associations were acceptable to many Israelites. However, there are indications that in the late Second Temple Period, many Jews did consider any physical contact with Gentiles or Gentile things defiling. In the first-century BCE text *Judith*, Judith, after leaving the Gentile Holofernes's camp, immersed in a spring to purify herself from Gentile defilement (Jdt 12:6–9). Later Rabbinic tradition also refers to Gentiles and goods they produce (such as oil or wine) as ritually defiling.

36. Jacob Milgrom, "The Dynamics of Purity in the Priestly System," in *Purity and Holiness: The Heritage of Leviticus*, ed. M. J. H. M. Poorthuis and J. Schwartz (Leiden, Brill, 2000), 31.

in intertestamental traditions (e.g., Judith, 1 Maccabees), Qumran texts, Philo, Josephus, New Testament, and rabbinic writings, it seems likely that the Levitical and Deuteronomic identifications of which animals could and could not be eaten were also followed by many Israelites of this era (see Leviticus 11; Deuteronomy 14). In these traditions, all of the animals listed are classified as either clean and allowed for food, or unclean and forbidden, though no animal imparts impurity while it is alive. As Douglas explains, "impure means that their corpses render unclean the person who makes contact, and thus calls for a sacrifice of expiation."[37] In summary, all sea creatures with fins or scales are allowed as food. All land creatures meeting all three criteria—divided hoofs, cleft-footed, and chewing the cud—are allowed for food and for sacrifices (most animals domesticated by Israelites fit this category). Several species of birds are not allowed, many of them raptors or scavengers (see Lev 11:13–19), and most insects are not allowed, except the locust, the bald locust, the cricket, and the grasshopper. Israelites were also prohibited from consuming blood. Thus, they were to drain the blood from the animal prior to preparing its meat for food or as part of the process of offering it on the altar, and cover it with earth (Lev 17:10–14). We saw above that the use of stone vessels to safeguard food and handlers from impurity was seemingly common among Israelite folk by the end of the Second Temple Period. By the time we get to Jesus's day, it is also clear that Pharisees among others are washing prior to consuming food and have developed rituals for the washing of vessels (e.g., Mark 7). These notices from the gospels add further credence to reports in Rabbinic tradition that some Pharisees, among others, sought to eat ordinary food in a state of ritual purity, as priests would do when consuming ritual offerings.[38]

Therefore, this convergence of textual and archaeological data strongly suggests that many Israelites during this period wove purity practices and rituals into their daily lives. Insights from cultural anthropology help us offer some informed speculation on the motivations behind the expansion of these purity practices among Israelites living in the land of Israel in the late Second Temple Period. The cross-cultural anthropological studies featured in the Frevel and Nihan volume indicate that purity practices often undergo development during periods of social

---

37. Mary Douglas, "Impurity of Land Animals," in *Purity and Holiness*, ed. Poorthuis and Schwartz, 40.

38. See Miller, *Texts and Material Finds*, 215–23; Jonathan Brumberg-Kraus, Susan Marks, and Jordan D. Rosenblum, "Ten Theses Concerning Meals and Early Judaism," in *Meals in Early Judaism: Social Formation at the Table*, ed. Susan Marks and Hal Tausig (New York: Palgrave Macmillan, 2014), 24.

and political upheaval. The suffering of Israelites under the Seleucids followed by the protracted Maccabean revolt in the mid-second century BCE, the civil wars of the Hasmonean era leading to Pompey's invasion of Jerusalem in 64 BCE, the destruction and enslavement of thousands that resulted from that invasion, and the marked change in Israel's status from an independent to occupied nation, would all likely provide suitable contexts for the intensification and development of purity conceptions and practices. It is reasonable to expect that in the aftermath of these events, various Israelite groups in the land of Israel might look to purity practices to further distinguish themselves as Jews vis-à-vis their Greek and then Roman conquerors and occupiers.

As we also learned from Frevel and Nihan above, "the opposition between pure and impure serves first and foremost to define a key aspect of the relationship between human beings (male and female) and deities, which can then be used, so to speak, in a derivative manner, in order to construe and conceptualize the relationships between in-group and out-group, or within the group itself."[39] Therefore, it also makes sense that some Jews during these volatile periods would use purity as a mechanism of social differentiation *within* the Israelite community. This had already been the case for centuries among the aristocratic, priestly class, who served as the "ritual specialists" qualified to distinguish between pure and impure and enact the rituals that can return persons to purity. But in the first century BCE, the covenanters at Qumran embraced their own form of intense purity practices as a mechanism of radical differentiation from their fellow Israelites. Segregating themselves in the Judean wilderness, they were the one, true Israel, awaiting the establishment of the heavenly temple and righteous priesthood to replace the defiled temple and sham priesthood currently standing in Jerusalem.

The expansion of purity among common Israelites, many of whom did not belong to a particular group or sect beyond their kinship relations, may also have been motivated in varying degrees by a sense of threat and loss of control due to Roman hegemony and insults against Jewish sensibilities. Moreover, common folk may have found it particularly meaningful to reestablish a sense of everyday holiness, a daily experience of connection to God and to authentic community based on more local, ancestral traditions and apart from the Israelite religious establishment. Perhaps they were searching for a way to define their relationship to God, one another, and creation that bypassed the very costly brokerage levied against them by the religious specialists of the temple cult. Our review of the first-century CE Roman world in chap-

39. Miller, *Texts and Material Finds*, 37.

ters 2–3, aided by the input of cultural anthropology, helped us to see the widespread social, political, and economic subjugation of the masses by the elite, including the Israelite elite governing the temple. Moreover, the Qumran community provides us an example of Israelites condemning the temple elite for their greed and collusion with their Roman oppressors and establishing their own purity conceptions and practices in response.[40] As we shall see, the New Testament gospels offer a similar critique. Such critique would not have been an innovation of Israelites during this period. It had already been a long-standing part of Israelite tradition. After reviewing the criticism of the Temple and priesthood found in Jeremiah's temple sermon and the final chapters of Ezekiel, Klawans concludes:

> Sacrifice became anathema for the prophets not because God preferred a loftier form of worship, not because the Temple service was performed by people who had other things on their minds. The prophetic critique of contemporary cultic practice stemmed from the fact that many sacrifices were being offered by those whose property was unduly earned, being proceeds from the exploitation of the poor.[41]

In sum, these first-century manifestations of antipathy toward the temple establishment may reflect a rather widespread sentiment among Israelites during this period, who may have turned to practices of purity to forge their own nonbrokered access to God.

Such "grassroots" purity movements would likely have been characterized by a rather high degree of variability. Two factors suggest this. As we saw above, the exploitative economic system regulated by Rome and facilitated by the temple elite left the vast majority of the population living at the precarious edge of subsistence, with anywhere from 30 to 40 percent of the population in the land of Israel subjected to slavery. Thus, one major factor motivating many Israelites to seek an authentic religious life apart from the very same authorities contributing to their deprivation also made the practice of purity challenging in some important respects. For a family experiencing malnutrition, protein would be welcome no matter the source. Similarly, while *mikva'ot* appear to be fairly widespread, public pools may not exist in every village or town, and only a fraction of Israelites had one attached to their dwelling. Agricultural workers may not have been able to wash before consum-

40. See Catherine M. Murphy, *Wealth in the Dead Sea Scrolls and in the Qumran Community*, Studies on the Texts of the Desert of Judah 40 (Leiden: Brill, 2002); Jonathan Klawans, *Purity, Sacrifice, and the Temple: Symbolism and Supersessionism in the Study of Ancient Judaism* (Oxford: Oxford University Press, 2006), 145–74.

41. Klawans, *Purity, Sacrifice, and the Temple*, 249.

ing foods while afield and slaves may not have had the liberty to engage in regular ablutions. A second factor contributing to the variability of purity practices among Jews was that it was largely unregulated and based on traditions open to varying interpretations when it came to specific practices. To be sure, there were Jewish associations that had developed, labeled *haverim* by Josephus and the Rabbis, which sought to define and practice purity rules with an uncommon degree of specificity and rigidity. These associations, some comprised of Pharisees, may have been an important component of the expansionist movement. But it is also likely that many Israelites would be resistant to expansionist practices that would label fellow kin members and longtime friends and associates as impure. Pharisaic purity practices, in other words, may have become *too* differentiating for common folk. What Kazen describes as typical for Galilee was just as probable throughout Judea: "Many common people living within the village economies of Galilee could neither afford nor accept expansionist solutions that would affect social relationships and the tight-knit pattern of the extended family which were as much a part of the ancestral tradition as well."[42] Such resistance would also be likely if these associations of *haverim* were claiming an authority to redefine and regulate the purity practices of the underclass, which developed, in part, to seek a communion with God unregulated by self-asserted powerbrokers.

THE ROLE OF THE PHARISEES IN PROMOTING PURITY PRACTICES IN THE FIRST CENTURY CE

The Pharisees were not separatists like the covenanters of Qumran. They remained thoroughly integrated in Israelite society and seemed to focus their mission among the common folk of town and village. According to Josephus, early Rabbinic tradition, and the NT writings, the Pharisees stressed devotion to Israelite law in everyday life, particularly in the matters of Sabbath observance, tithing to the temple, and purity. While there were undoubtedly variations among their members, some Pharisees required elements of priestly ritual purity for themselves and all righteous Jews, along with other stipulations not found in the Torah, such as eating meals in a state of ritual purity. As mentioned above, some Pharisees grouped themselves into *haverim*, associations dedicated to the practice of purity, which likely functioned as a fictive kinship group and helped them practice and promote their ideals. As reflected in Rabbinic

42. Kazen, *Jesus and Purity*, 293.

traditions, at least some Pharisees (and Rabbis) referred to Israelites who neglected to implement their stringent purity practices as 'Am-ha'aretz, "people of the land." Although this is not by itself a derogatory term, the implication in contrast to Pharisaic practice and status is that those belonging to this grouping were to be considered impure and at best marginal members of True Israel. While the Pharisees became strident advocates for the expansion of purity practices, it is hard to say whether or not they played a role in initiating this expansion or rather sought to mold and control it after it was well underway. In either case, they too used purity as a means of differentiation. It appears that at least some Pharisees also used purity as a means of status enhancement. Eyal Regev speculates that the Pharisees, having lost significant power and influence during the rise of Herod, turned to purity-driven honor to compete with the status of the priesthood and win the admiration of the people.[43] If so, they may have been aided in their pursuits by the common folks' antipathy for the priestly elite..

Other scholars, based on a reading of the gospel traditions informed by social-scientific analysis and the social, economic, and political character of Roman Palestine we reviewed in chapters 2–3, propose another explanation for the Pharisaic focus on purity. They argue that the Pharisees served in a retainer-like role relative to the priestly aristocrats overseeing the temple.[44] As mentioned above, Pharisees zealously promoted tithing to the temple, and included the practice as a central ritual of common meals. William Herzog argues that a "debt code" had become established within Second Temple Israelite society as a mechanism for supporting the temple and cult. The theological rationale behind this code was that offerings to the temple were really offerings to God, in gratitude for the blessings that God had bestowed upon God's people: "it fulfilled important prescriptions for maintaining a healthy relationship with the God who called the people into existence and made them a great nation."[45] However, it also placed serious economic pressure on peasants, who often had to scrounge to make the tax payments. Under Roman occupation, the tax burden on the peasant class became even more extreme, possibly reaching over 40 percent, temple and Roman

43. See Regev, "Pure Individualism: The Idea of Non-Priestly Purity in Ancient Judaism," *Journal for the Study of Judaism* 31 (2000): 195.

44. See William R. Herzog II, *Parables as Subversive Speech: Jesus as Pedagogue of the Oppressed* (Louisville: Westminster John Knox, 1994), 178–89; Lawrence M. Wills, *Not God's People: Insiders and Outsiders in the Biblical World* (New York: Rowman & Littlefield, 2008), 106; Kazen, *Jesus and Purity*, 298; Malina and Pilch, *Social-Science Commentary*, 382–83; Dieter Heinrich Reinstorf, "The Rich, the Poor, and the Law," *HTS* 60, no. 1/2 (2004): 329–48.

45. Herzog, *Parables*, 179.

taxes combined.[46] As Herzog reports, "The Temple system was no less oppressive than Roman occupation, but the combination of the two systems of tribute produced a crisis among the peasant population base."[47] As a result, the debt code, which had as its initial rationale the expression of gratitude to God for God's blessing upon the whole of Israelite society, including the poor and marginalized, had become the means by which Israel's elite extracted resources from the poor and pushed them toward destitution in order to maintain their own wealth and social position. The Pharisees, Herzog argues, introduced a theological innovation to assist the exploitative temple economy:

> Essentially, the scribal Pharisees made the debt code a function of the purity code. The failure to pay tithes rendered one impure, and once impure, one remained forever in debt, unable to satisfy the demands of redemptive media. This theological move was made to support the economic base of the Temple in Jerusalem, which was dependent on agricultural tithes. The move ignored the reasons the people of the land were unable to pay their tributary tithes to the Temple by increasing pressure on them to do so and stigmatizing them for their failure. It also conveniently overlooked the role of the Temple as an institution of extension [i.e., extending God's grace and blessing] by converting it into an institution of accumulation. In the process, debt became a form of impurity.[48]

This theory is a good example of how biblical scholars utilize the insights of cultural anthropology to understand with more precision the complex social, political, religious, and economic contexts of the biblical writings, and in doing so create new avenues for interpretation. What also makes this theory attractive, in my view, is that it coheres closely with two related findings from the Frevel and Nihan volume noted above. The first is that purity-related stigmatization is frequently aimed at internal differentiation and, among Israelites in particular, likely results from disagreements on the defining markers of Judaism. Second, there is also a tendency within Mediterranean traditions during this time, and again especially within Judaism, to merge together what had been distinct forms of purity (such as ritual/physical and moral purity). To these more generalized concepts of purity are then added new conceptions of pollution as an attempt to stigmatize others and further differentiate one's group from them. Both of these tendencies are clearly reflected in the

---

46. See Reinstorf, "The Rich, the Poor, and the Law," 337–41 for a helpful and concise detailing of the Roman and temple-related taxations imposed on Israelites in the first century.

47. Herzog, *Parables*, 181.

48. Herzog, *Parables*, 184.

proposed Pharisaic innovation of labeling failure to tithe as a failure to uphold divinely ordered purity norms.

The gospels do indeed portray the Pharisees as heavy-handedly imposing purity practices on those they sought to enlighten, using purity as a means of honor enhancement, promoting tithing as a form of exploitation, and embracing the elite values of greed and self-importance. For a rather intense, but representative example of this characterization, see the woes of Matthew 23:1–36 and Luke 11:37–53. Numerous scholars have argued that the gospels' portrayal of the Pharisees is imbalanced and prejudicial. It arises out of a polemical context emerging between Christian and non-Christian Jews in the post-70 CE world after the fall of Jerusalem and destruction of the Temple, and is not an accurate representation of the Pharisaic movement in Jesus's day. It is indeed possible that the gospels' portrayals of the Pharisees overstate or misrepresent elements of their character and mission. There are a few passages that present Pharisees in a somewhat positive light (e.g., John 3:1–10; 19:39; Luke 13:31), and Luke tells us that Pharisees (including Paul!) joined the early Jesus movement (Acts 15:5; cf. Phil 3:5). Yet on the whole, the gospels cast the Pharisees as unified in their opposition to the mission of Jesus and the values of the kingdom. At the very least, the gospels' portraits likely emerge out of polemical contexts and emphasize what the early church would find most problematic about the Pharisees. Still, it is also possible that the portrait provided by the gospels in many respects accurately captures the tendencies of Jesus's Pharisaic opponents. As J. Neusner concludes, "The Gospel's picture conforms to the rabbinical traditions about the Pharisees, which center upon the laws of tithing and ritual purity, defining what and with whom one may eat, that is, table fellowship."[49] Moreover, that Pharisees would use purity practices as a means of social differentiation and status enhancement relative to the people of the land is (as I just noted) also consistent with our understanding of purity practices within the Mediterranean world as informed by the cross-cultural analysis we reviewed above, and the social characteristics of that world as informed by cultural anthropology. While the Pharisees may not have initiated the expansion of nonpriestly piety among many Israelites, some of them may have sought to co-opt those practices, imposing further rigidity and specificity, connecting tithing with purity to facilitate their role as retainers, and elevating themselves as paragons to be followed. This would also be entirely consistent with the common

---

49. Jacob Neusner, *From Politics to Piety: The Emergence of Pharisaic Judaism* (Eugene, OR: Wipf & Stock, 1979), 80.

marriage of political, economic, and religious authority in the ancient Mediterranean as unveiled by cultural anthropology.

JESUS'S RESPONSE TO THE PHARISEES AND THEIR CONCEPTIONS OF PURITY AS PORTRAYED BY THE GOSPELS

The theory I described above promoted by Herzog and others has much to commend it, for it makes sense of the variable practice of purity in the Judaism of this time and the wider Mediterranean world, and of the portrayal of the Pharisees within the gospels and other ancient sources.[50] Again, the use of purity for the purpose of stigmatization is common within purity-oriented cultures especially during periods when defining markers of cultural identity are in dispute. Thus, one could safely assume that there were many peasants (and other Israelites) during this time in Judaism who disputed the notion that inability to pay temple-related tithes and taxes conferred impurity. There were also likely many who believed that the Pharisees were not reliable guides on how purity was to be pursued by faithful Israelites. The gospels portray Jesus as among them. Each of the gospels shapes Jesus's response to the Pharisees and their understanding of purity in somewhat different hues. In what follows, I will lean on Luke's account as a representative case, and even here I will strive to be concise. The objective will not be to provide an exhaustive review of Luke's portrait but to continue demonstrating how the insights of cultural anthropology may be helpful for examining this matter.

To structure our account of Luke's portrayal of Jesus's views on purity, I will return to a version of the purity maps we introduced earlier in this chapter to guide the way.[51] I will seek to plot out Jesus's symbolic maps of things in their proper place so that God's blessing may prevail for humanity and the rest of creation, in comparison to the mapping

50. I will limit my discussion here to the portrayal of Jesus's interaction with the Pharisees provided by the gospels (specifically Luke) and not venture into the troubled waters of trying to determine how accurately that portrait conveys a "historical Jesus." Beyond space considerations, I offer two reasons for this limitation. First, in my judgment the methodologies scholars employ to ferret out authentic sayings and actions of Jesus from the gospels are problematic to the point of being seriously deficient. They are simply inadequate to the task, leading to the reality that imaginative speculation much more than reliable data is the actual driver of such reconstructions. Second, I believe that the biblical scholars engaged in these endeavors have yet to show that the gospels' portraits of Jesus are largely nonhistorical and inaccurate. In fact, many of them simply assume it as a methodological starting point (e.g., the criterion of dissimilarity).

51. See pp. 96–99 above. I am borrowing and adapting this technique from Neyrey, "Symbolic Universe of Luke–Acts," 285–89.

strategies of the Pharisees. Once again, however, I want to caution the reader that the Pharisaic movement was itself likely variable, and I do not intend to imply that Luke's portrait of Jesus's opponents as presented here was true of all Pharisees in his or Jesus's day. Two additional cautions are in order as we move ahead. I think it is common for Christian readers of the NT to conclude that Jesus ran roughshod over Israelite purity norms and intended to marginalize, if not eliminate, their significance for his fellow Jews (e.g., Mark 7:1–23). As we shall see, Luke does present Jesus as practicing purity in ways that markedly differ from that of the Pharisees with whom he was engaged. Yet I think a more accurate characterization—which I present below—is that Jesus did not eliminate these purity maps of his fellow Jews as much as he followed and implemented them guided by a very different point of orientation. Also, many Christians have framed these disputes as Jesus—modeling a Christian viewpoint—revealing the waywardness of the Pharisaic, namely Jewish, viewpoint on the matter of law observance. Such a reading is anachronistic and misrepresents the context for these debates, which was a thoroughly intra-Jewish one, both in Jesus's day and very likely in the evangelists' day.[52] It is also a reading that has tragically fueled much anti-Semitism among Christians in the centuries following these debates, including our own.

Maps of Time

In Israelite tradition, maps of time specified rules for the Sabbath, observance of festivals, and when circumcision should be performed. While Jesus wrangles with the Pharisees over proper Sabbath-keeping, Luke shows Jesus and his family following key elements of the Israelite map of time. Jesus was circumcised on his eighth day (2:21) and presented in the temple "when the time came for their purification" (2:22–24). His family traveled to Jerusalem for the Passover "every year" (2:41), a practice he apparently maintained (22:1). Jesus's first public act recorded by Luke is set in his hometown synagogue in Nazareth, where he went "on the Sabbath day, as was his custom" (4:16). However, much to the Pharisees' consternation, Jesus performed what they considered work on the Sabbath, allowing his hungry disciples to glean grain as they walked

---

52. I doubt that many of the particular purity codes Jesus and the Pharisees wrangled over were of central concern to most Gentile converts to the Jesus movement, even though some Gentile Christians may have been drawn into these debates among Jewish Christians and between Christian and non-Christian Jews (e.g., Galatians). I also think it likely that all of the gospel writers were Israelite, including Luke. See Karl Kuhn, *The Kingdom according to Luke and Acts* (Grand Rapids: Baker Academic, 2015), 60–63.

through a field (6:1–5), healing a man with a withered hand (6:6–11) and later a crippled woman (13:10–17). Jesus also apparently neglected the practice of fasting (5:33–38). Jesus's responses to the Pharisees during these disputes on Sabbath-keeping share a common theme: addressing the essential needs of human well-being is the proper practice of Sabbath. Put another way, action or nonaction that neglects basic human need and well-being is out of place at all times, but *especially* on the Sabbath. I think we can validly speculate how Jesus's responses and map of Sabbath time are symbolic of his (very traditional!) worldview. Sabbath was meant to celebrate God's gift of blessing in and through creation (see Gen 2:1–3; Exod 20:8–11) and to commemorate God's deliverance of Israel from bondage (see Deut 5:12–15). To fail to address human deprivation, enslavement, and suffering (see Luke 13:15–16) on the Sabbath was to act in a manner diametrically opposed to its purpose. As "Lord of the Sabbath" (6:5) Jesus possesses the authority to recast Sabbath-keeping in a manner consistent with God's holiness—God's identity as Creator and Savior.

Maps of Places

What spaces did Jesus regard as sacred? As noted above, Jesus and his parents appear in the temple for his dedication. Years later but still a child, Jesus slips away from his family as they set off for home to return from their annual pilgrimage to Jerusalem. He spends several days in "his father's house," before Mary and Joseph locate him and take him back to Nazareth (2:41–51). Jesus mourns over Jerusalem and the temple as he prophesizes its destruction at the hands of the Romans (19:41–44), and then he proceeds to drive out those exchanging money and selling sacrificial animals on behalf of the elite (19:45–46). As noted above, Jesus regularly attended synagogue, and his followers after him preached both in the temple precincts and local synagogues. For Jesus, the temple and synagogue were indeed sacred spaces.

Yet as we saw in chapter 4, the angelic announcement of Lord Messiah Jesus's birth comes not to the elite in the temple but to shepherds in the fields (2:8–20). Jesus also ministers outside of the land of Israel among Samaritans (9:51–56) and to Gentiles (7:1–10; 8:26–39) and calls his followers to spread the message of the kingdom's arrival "to the ends of the earth" (Acts 1:8). Therefore, Luke shows Jesus honoring temple, synagogue, and Israel as sacred, but not inviolably or exclusively so. Like the covenanters of Qumran, Jesus regarded the current temple leadership as unfaithful and saw the current temple structure and Jerusalem itself as headed toward ruin (Luke 13:34–45; 19:41–44; 21:20–24). Jesus honored the role these sacred spaces served for the purpose of making Israel a holy people, but the ability of these locales to function as sacred space had become severely compromised by those charged with their maintenance. Rather than facilitating the maturation of Israel into the blessed and holy people of God, they had become "dens of robbers" and haunts of those who "devour widow's houses" (20:47), and the city of those who slayed the prophets (19:49–50).

From Luke's perspective, the degradation—the *impurity* even—of these sacred spaces is indeed tragic.[53] But these sacred spaces do not exhaust God's opportunity to be present with and deliver God's people, and even all of humanity. Ultimately—in the words of Jesus's disciple Stephen—"the Most High does not dwell in houses made with human hands" (Acts 7:48). Luke reveals throughout the gospel and Acts that God's Spirit is able to transform profane and even defiled places into sacred space where God's presence and blessing are encountered. In other words, sacred space, for Luke, is no longer a function of *place*, but a function of the *Spirit's ministry*. God's holiness, God's merciful blessing as Sovereign Creator, and the advent of God's kingdom, are not circumscribed by structures wrought by human hands but can be encountered in places as diverse and defiled as the temple, synagogues, Israelite homes, Gentile homes, fields, wilderness, squalid city streets, dusty country roads, graveyards, and even a Roman cross.

Maps of Persons and Meals

Just as God's mercy and blessing can be encountered in spaces formerly mapped as profane or defiled, so too can God's mercy and blessing be encountered by *and through* those typically mapped in Jesus's context as profane or defiled. As we saw above, at least some Pharisees would have avoided contact with anyone not practicing purity as they defined it or otherwise unclean, such as publicly known "sinners," those unable to pay their temple taxes, those suffering from scale disease and flows of menstrual blood, demoniacs, the dead, and especially Gentiles. Moreover, many ill people were regarded as suffering from an "unclean spirit," and Pharisees would have likely steered clear of these as well. The Pharisees' map of persons, in other words, was utilized for the purpose of separation, avoidance, and as we saw above, stigmatization of others and

53. On the tragic dimension of Luke's account, see Robert C. Tannehill, *The Narrative Unity of Luke–Acts: A Literary Interpretation* (Minneapolis: Fortress Press, 1986, 1990), 2.344–57; Kuhn, *Kingdom according to Luke and Acts*, 272–73.

their own status enhancement. Luke's portrait affirms this: e.g., "God, I thank you that I am not like other people: thieves, rogues, adulterers, or even like this tax collector!" (18:11). While the Pharisees avoided and denigrated marginal persons as a means of leveraging their own honor, Jesus engaged and elevated the marginalized, while challenging those who degraded them. The theme of reversal is one of the most prominent coursing throughout Luke's two-volume work. Mary's Song (1:46–55), the calling of the disciples (5:1–11, 27–32), the blessing and woes of Jesus's sermon on the plain (6:22–26), followed by his call to love enemies (6:27–36), his castigation of the Pharisees and lawyers (11:37–52), and Peter's visit to the home of Cornelius (Acts 10) are among notable manifestations of the motif. Joining these passages are scores of others in which Jesus provides healing and wholeness to those suffering defilements of various sorts, such as the dead (7:11–17; 8:54–55), the scaled (5:13), the bleeding (8:44), the possessed, including a Gentile (4:31–37; 8:26–35), and the sinful (7:47; 19:1–10). Jesus shared with his fellow Jews the recognition that these sinners and sufferers were indeed "out of place." But he responded to them with mercy and the gift of wholeness, not the callous disregard displayed by the Pharisees and other elites. He rejected their marginalized status and instead welcomed them as cherished kin into God's kingdom.

Similarly, Jesus's meal practices similarly reveal a very different orientation toward others than the meal practices enacted by some Pharisees. Jesus shared with the Pharisees the notion that meals were meant to enact authentic community as they celebrated God's provision and bore witness to what is good and pure. Yet in contrast to the highly guarded nature of Pharisaic meal practices, Jesus's table fellowship is radically inclusive, as Jesus shares table with characters of wildly varied backgrounds and social locations, including those whom many label as "sinners" (e.g., 5:30; 7:34, 37; 19:1–10). Moreover, Jesus's table-talk during the meals he attends parallels his table manners and the company he keeps. Jesus uses these meal scenes as occasions to teach about the true values of the kingdom and the radical reorientation of perspective that life in the kingdom demands. Frequently, Jesus challenges the honor, status, and purity concerns governing such meals and their hosts, and unveils actions and dispositions that reflect a mind and heart open to God's reign, such as humility, repentance, and gratitude (e.g., 7:36–50; 11:37–54; 14:1–24; 19:1–10). Luke's table scenes also express important elements of his Christology. They present Jesus as a provider, or savior, either as one presiding over the meal or as one who offers God's healing and provision to others during the meal. In sum, Luke's meal scenes present Jesus—often in contrast to the Pharisees and elite—as the provider of the kind of fare and community that lead to true blessing.

The Center of Jesus's Symbolic World

In light of this review of Jesus's mapping of time, space, persons, and meals, a critical point to appreciate is that Jesus did not simply "do away with" the purity codes of his fellow Israelites. Informed by cultural anthropology, we have seen that purity concepts and practices define what is proper, what fits, and what belongs. They shape and give expression to the maps we use to make sense of the world and navigate our relations to the gods, persons, places, and things within it. And if we look carefully, we find that Jesus shared many of the main mapping strategies of his fellow Israelites, at least in terms of their broad contours. Israelite maps of time were important to Jesus, including Sabbath, rites of passage, and other festivals remembering and celebrating God's sovereignty and intentions for Israel and the world. Jesus also honored space that was sacred to his fellow Israelites. Though he foresaw the impending destruction of Jerusalem and the temple, he—like Israelite prophets before him—lamented the destruction of his "father's house" as nothing less than tragic, representing the defilement of these sacred spaces due to the greed, thievery, and depravity of those called to steward God's bounty and mercy. Jesus shared his fellow Israelites' views that disease, possession, disfigurement, sinful lifestyles, and being outside the community of God's people, made one "out of place." He also shared with his Pharisee hosts that the meals they celebrate should bear witness to the abundant provision and holiness of God.

But we can also see, from Luke's vantage point at least, that Jesus's mapping of time, place, people, and meals revolved around a very different point of orientation than did the mapping strategies of his Pharisaic detractors. Jesus and the Pharisees may have had similar maps, but they navigated them with a radically different compass. To try another analogy, Jesus belonged to a stratum of Judaism that inhabited a "parallel universe" in which so much was the same but at the same time also fundamentally different from the universe inhabited by these fellow Israelites. In Jesus's world, Israel's holiness, its "set-apartness," served not as a sign of Israel's exclusive access to God and elevated worthiness before God. Rather, Jesus saw Israel's holiness, "set-apartness," as Israel's calling to *enact God's blessing and deliverance*, to bear witness to the holiness of God and invite *all* persons to return to God's presence and embrace the wholeness radiating out from God's reign among them.

As we have already seen, this orientation to Jesus's map was as ancient as Jesus's ancestor, Abram: "and in you all nations of the earth shall be blessed" (Gen 12:3). It was an orientation we find coursing throughout Israel's sacred traditions during those moments when Israel takes up its calling as a "Priestly Kingdom" and "Holy Nation" (Exod 19:1–6). It was an orientation reclaimed by the prophets whose words are recorded in Isaiah 56 and Malachi, and the stories of Ruth and Jonah, in response to the genealogical purity codes mandated by Ezra and Nehemiah. But it was also an orientation that many of Jesus's fellow Israelites were unwilling to follow. This too, from Luke's perspective, was nothing less than tragic. And it was certainly "out of place" in God's new kingdom.

RETURNING TO LUKE 7

We are at a meal. And again, Jesus uses it as an occasion to teach, to urge his fellow Israelites to embrace an orientation toward God and others that will enable them to welcome the arrival of God's long-awaited reign. Remember the scene. A woman, a "sinful" woman, enters the sacred space of a Pharisee's home while dinner is on the table. Alarm and consternation flash from face to face. And then this contagion of a woman falls over, fawns over, slobbers over, washes over, Jesus. Alarm morphs into disgust. "If this man were a prophet! He would know! She is *unclean*! This is not right!"

But the wrongness of that moment, the "out-of-place-ness" of that moment, was not with the woman, or with Jesus. "Simon, I have something to say to you." And at least Simon knew enough to reply, "Teacher, speak." In the words Jesus offers, he tries to help Simon see his own impurity through parable, and the woman through her acts of love and devotion: to see her not as a contagion but as a model of true purity to emulate! The wrongness of that moment was that Simon was unaware that the mapping he was using to guide his relations with God and others could only lead to his separation from God and others (see Luke 16:19–31). Simon, simply yet tragically, did not have the right orientation point for calibrating a proper sense of the holy. Holiness, Jesus tries to show Simon and his fellow *haverim*, was first and foremost mercy and love for the other, even ones as defiled and out of place as this woman, the deformed, those Gentiles, and your enemies. "You shall be holy, for I the Lord your God am holy" (Lev 19:2). For Jesus, this meant "Be merciful, just as your Father is merciful" (Luke 6:36).

CONCLUSION

Though challenging, the topic of purity was perhaps a useful one for concluding our discussion on the insights cultural anthropology can offer readers of Scripture. The large-scale model evolving from the work of Mary Douglas that views purity codes and practices as symbolic expressions of the maps people use to order themselves in relation to the world provided the framework for our investigation. From this paradigm we utilized the maps of time, place, persons, things, and foods/meals as models for exploring the purity practice of Israelites in the late Second Temple Period and the symbolic world of Jesus in relation to that of the Pharisees as portrayed in the gospels. We drew from the recent cross-cultural studies provided by Frevel and Nihan, whose overview of commonalities in the purity conceptions and practices of various Mediterranean cultures provided important touchstones for our analysis. We also continued to benefit from our review in chapters 2 and 3 of the common social, political, and economic characteristics of the Roman Mediterranean world as illuminated by cultural anthropology—a world of steep social and economic stratification, widespread deprivation among peasants and slaves, and agonistic social relations, especially among the elite—to shape our understanding of the nature of the Pharisaic movement and the conflict between some of its members and Jesus. In this chapter, as in the ones preceding it, our goal has been to illustrate how cultural anthropology enables readers of Scripture to delve more deeply and perceptively into the contexts from which the biblical traditions emerged so that our interpretive endeavors may fly truer and land nearer the mark.

Bibliography

Adams, Samuel L. *Social and Economic Life in Second Temple Judea*. Louisville: Westminster John Knox, 2014.

Adler, Yonatan. "Jewish Purity Practices in Roman Judea: The Evidence of Archaeology." ASOR Blog, February 2017. https://tinyurl.com/y78xd6c.

———. "Between Priestly Cult and Common Culture: The Material Evidence of Ritual Purity Observance in Early Roman Jerusalem Reassessed." *Journal of Ancient Judaism* 7 (2016): 228–48.

Bock, Darrell L. *Luke 1:1–9:50*. BECNT. Grand Rapids: Baker Academic, 1994.

Bovon, François. *Luke 1: A Commentary on the Gospel of Luke 1:1–9:50*. Hermeneia. Minneapolis: Fortress Press, 2002.

Brown, Raymond E. *The Birth of the Messiah: A Commentary on the Infancy Narratives in the Gospels of Matthew and Luke*. Rev. ed. New York: Doubleday, 1993.

Brumberg-Kraus, Jonathan, Susan Marks, and Jordan D. Rosenblum. "Ten Theses Concerning Meals and Early Judaism." In *Meals in Early Judaism: Social Formation at the Table*, edited by Susan Marks and Hal Tausig, 13–39. New York: Palgrave Macmillan, 2014.

Carter, T. L. "The Irony of Romans 13." *NovT* 46 (2004): 209–28.

Carter, Warren. *The Roman Empire and the New Testament: An Essential Guide*. Abingdon Essential Guides. Nashville: Abingdon, 2006.

Crapo, Richley. *Cultural Anthropology: Understanding Ourselves and Others*. 5th ed. Boston: McGraw-Hill, 2002.

Douglas, Mary. *Purity and Danger: An Analysis of the Concepts of Pollution and Taboo*. London: Routledge & Kegan Paul, 1966, 2002.

———. *Implicit Meanings: Mary Douglas: Collected Works*. New York: Routledge, 1975, 2003.

———. "Impurity of Land Animals." In *Purity and Holiness: The Heritage of Leviticus*, edited by M. J. H. M. Poorthuis and J. Schwartz, 33–46. Leiden, Brill, 2000.

Ego, Beate. "Purity Concepts in Jewish Traditions of the Hellenistic Period." In *Purity and the Forming of Religious Traditions in the Ancient Mediterranean World and Ancient Judaism*, edited by Christian Frevel and Christophe Nihan, 477–92. Leiden: Brill, 2013.

Elliot, John H. *What Is Social-Scientific Criticism?* Edited by Dan O. Via Jr. Guides to Biblical Scholarship. Minneapolis: Fortress Press, 1993.

Elliott, Neil. *The Arrogance of the Nations: Reading Romans in the Shadow of Empire*. Paul in Critical Contexts Series. Minneapolis: Fortress Press, 2008.

Esler, Philip F., ed. *Modelling Early Christianity: Social-Scientific Studies of the New Testament in Its Context*. New York: Routledge, 1995.

———. "Introduction: Models, Context and Kerygma in New Testament Interpretation." In *Modelling Early Christianity: Social-Scientific Studies of the New Testament in Its Context*, edited by Philip F. Esler, 1–22. New York: Routledge, 1995.

Ferraro, Gary, and Susan Andreatta. *Cultural Anthropology: An Applied Perspective*. 10th ed. Stamford, CT: Cengage, 2014.

Fiensy, David A. *The Social History of Palestine in the Herodian Period: The Land Is Mine*. Studies in the Bible and Early Christianity 20. Lewiston, NY: Edwin Mellen, 1991.

Fitzmyer, Joseph A. *The Gospel According to Luke I–IX*. AB 28. New York: Doubleday, 1981.

Frevel, Christian. "Purity Conceptions in the Book of Numbers in Context." In *Purity and the Forming of Religious Traditions in the Ancient Mediterranean World and Ancient Judaism*, edited by Christian Freval and Christophe Nihan, 369–413. Leiden: Brill, 2013.

Frevel, Christian, and Christophe Nihan, eds. *Purity and the Forming of Religious Traditions in the Ancient Mediterranean World and Ancient Judaism*. Leiden: Brill, 2013.

———. Introduction to *Purity and the Forming of Religious Traditions in the Ancient Mediterranean World and Ancient Judaism*, edited by Christian Frevel and Christophe Nihan, 1–46. Leiden: Brill, 2013.

Green, Joel B. *The Gospel of Luke*. NICNT. Grand Rapids: Eerdmans, 1997.

Hamel, Gildas. "Poverty and Charity." In *The Oxford Handbook of Jewish Daily Life in Roman Palestine*, edited by Catherine Hezer, 308–26. Oxford: Oxford University Press, 2010.

Harland, Philip A. "The Economy of First-Century Palestine: State of the Scholarly Discussion." In *Handbook of Early Christianity: Social Science Approaches*, edited by Anthony J. Blasi et al., 511–27. Walnut Creek, CA: Alta Mira.

Hanson, K. C., and Douglas E. Oakman. *Palestine in the Time of Jesus: Social Structures and Social Conflicts*. 2nd ed. Minneapolis: Fortress Press, 1998.

Hays, Christine E. *Gentile Impurities and Jewish Identities: Intermarriage and Conversion from the Bible to the Talmud*. Oxford: Oxford University Press, 2002.

Herzog, William R., II. *Parables as Subversive Speech: Jesus as Pedagogue of the Oppressed*. Louisville: Westminster John Knox, 1994.

Hillers, Delbert R. *Micah: A Commentary on the Book of the Prophet Micah*. Hermeneia. Minneapolis: Fortress Press, 1988.

Hopkins, Keith. *Conquerors and Slaves*. Sociological Studies in Roman History. Cambridge: Cambridge University Press, 1978.

Horsley, Richard. *The Liberation of Christmas: The Infancy Narratives in Social Context*. Eugene, OR: Wipf & Stock, 1989.

———. "The Slave Systems of Classical Antiquity and Their Reluctant Recognition by Modern Scholars." *Semeia* 83/84 (1998): 19–66.

———. *Jesus and the Powers: Conflict, Covenant, and the Hope of the Poor*. Minneapolis: Fortress Press, 2011.

Jewett, Robert. *Romans: A Commentary*. Hermeneia. Minneapolis: Fortress Press, 2007.

Kazen, Thomas. *Jesus and Purity Halakhah: Was Jesus Indifferent to Impurity?* CB 38. Winona Lake, IN: Eisenbrauns, 2010.

Klawans, Jonathan. *Purity, Sacrifice, and the Temple: Symbolism and Supersessionism in the Study of Ancient Judaism*. Oxford: Oxford University Press, 2006.

Kuhn, Karl Allen. "Deaf or Defiant: The Literary, Cultural, and Affective-Rhetorical Keys to the Naming of John (Luke 1:57–80)." *CBQ* 75 (2013): 486–503.

———. *The Kingdom according to Luke and Acts*. Grand Rapids: Baker Academic, 2015.

Lavenda, Robert H., and Emily A. Schultz. *Core Concepts in Cultural Anthropology*. 5th ed. Boston: McGraw-Hill, 2013.

Lenski, Gerhard E. *Power and Privilege: A Theory of Social Stratification*. 2nd ed. Chapel Hill: University of North Carolina Press, 1984.

Magness, Jodi. *Stone and Dung, Oil and Spit: Jewish Daily Life in the Time of Jesus*. Grand Rapids: Eerdmans, 2011.

Malina, Bruce. "Early Christian Groups: Using Small Group Formation Theory to Explain Christian Organizations." In *Modelling Early Christianity: Social-Scientific Studies of the New Testament in Its Context*, edited by Philip F. Esler, 96–111. New York: Routledge, 1995.

———. *The New Testament World: Insights from Cultural Anthropology*. 3rd ed. Louisville: Westminster John Knox, 2001.

———. *The Social Gospel of Jesus: The Kingdom of God in Mediterranean Perspective*. Minneapolis: Fortress Press, 2001.

Malina, Bruce, and John Pilch. *Social-Science Commentary on the Letters of Paul*. Minneapolis: Fortress Press, 2006.

Marks, Susan, and Hal Taussig, eds. *Meals in Early Judaism: Social Formation at the Table*. New York: Palgrave Macmillan, 2014.

McCarthy, John D., and Mayer N. Zald. "Resource Mobilization and Social Movements: A Partial Theory." *American Journal of Sociology* 82, no. 6 (1977): 1212–41.

Milgrom, Jacob. "The Dynamics of Purity in the Priestly System." In *Purity and Holiness: The Heritage of Leviticus*, edited by M. J. H. M. Poorthuis and J. Schwartz, 29–32. Leiden, Brill, 2000.

Miller, Stuart. *At the Intersection of Texts and Material Finds: Stepped Pools, Stone Vessels and Ritual Purity among the Jews of Roman Galilee*. JAJSup 16. Göttingen: Vandenhoeck & Ruprecht, 2015.

Monoghan, John, and Peter Just. *Social and Cultural Anthropology: A Very Short Introduction*. Oxford: Oxford University Press, 2000.

Moulton, Harold K., ed. *The Analytical Greek Lexicon Revised*. Grand Rapids: Eerdmans, 1977.

Moxnes, Halvor. *The Economy of the Kingdom: Social Conflict and Economic Relations in Luke's Gospel*. Eugene, OR: Wipf & Stock, 1988.

Murphy, Catherine M. *Wealth in the Dead Sea Scrolls and in the Qumran Community*. Studies on the Texts of the Desert of Judah 40. Leiden: Brill, 2002.

Neff, David. "Misreading the Magnificat: It's Hard to Find Hymns that Embody Scripture's Sharp Critique of the Rich." *Christianity Today*, December 20, 2012. https://tinyurl.com/y78znyff.

Neusner, Jacob. *From Politics to Piety: The Emergence of Pharisaic Judaism*. Eugene, OR: Wipf & Stock, 1979.

Neyrey, Jerome, "The Symbolic Universe of Luke–Acts: 'They Turn the World Upside Down.'" In *The Social World of Luke–Acts: Models for Interpretation*, edited by Jerome Neyrey, 271–305. Peabody, MA: Hendrickson, 1991.

Nihan, Christophe. "Forms and Functions of Purity in Leviticus." In *Purity and the Forming of Religious Traditions in the Ancient Mediterranean World and Ancient Judaism*, edited by Christian Frevel and Christophe Nihan, 311–68. Leiden: Brill, 2013.

Nolland, John. *Luke 1–9:20*. WBC 35a. Waco, TX: Word, 1989.

Oakman, Douglas E. "Cursing Fig Trees and Robbers' Dens: Pronouncement Stories within Social-Systemic Perspective: Mark 11:12–15 and Parallels." *Semeia* 64 (1993): 253–72.

———. *Jesus and the Peasants*. Matrix: The Bible in Mediterranean Context. Eugene, OR: Cascade, 2008.

Poorthuis, M. J. H. M., and J. Schwartz, eds. *Purity and Holiness: The Heritage of Leviticus*. Leiden: Brill, 2000.

Price, S. R. F. *Rituals and Power: The Roman Imperial Cult in Asia Minor*. Cambridge: Cambridge University Press, 1984.

Rausche, Benedikt. "The Relevance of Purity in Second Temple Judaism according to Ezra–Nehemiah." In *Purity and the Forming of Religious Traditions in the Ancient Mediterranean World and Ancient Judaism*, edited by Christian Frevel and Christophe Nihan, 457–76. Leiden: Brill, 2013.

Regev, Eyal. "Pure Individualism: The Idea of Non-Priestly Purity in Ancient Judaism." *Journal for the Study of Judaism* 31 (2000): 176–202.

Reinstorf, Dieter Heinrich. "The Rich, the Poor, and the Law." *HTS* 60, no. 1/2 (2004): 329–48.

Rhoads, David. "Losing Life for Others in the Face of Death: Mark's Standards of Judgment." In *Gospel Interpretation: Narrative Critical & Social Scientific Approaches*, edited by Jack Dean Kingsbury, 83–94. Harrisburg, PA: Trinity Press International, 1997.

Rives, James B. *Religion in the Roman Empire*. Blackwell Ancient Religions 2. Oxford: Blackwell, 2007.

Robbins, Vernon K. "Social-Scientific Criticism and Literary Studies." In *Modelling Early Christianity: Social-Scientific Studies of the New Testament in Its Context*, edited by Philip F. Esler, 274–89. New York: Routledge, 1995.

Rohrbaugh, Richard. "The Social Location of the Markan Audience." In *The Social World of the New Testament: Insights and Models*, edited by Jerome H. Neyrey and Eric C. Stewart, 141–62. Peabody, MA: Hendrickson, 2008.

Rütersworden, Udo. "Purity Conceptions in Deuteronomy." In *Purity and the Forming of Religious Traditions in the Ancient Mediterranean World and Ancient Judaism*, edited by Christian Frevel and Christophe Nihan, 413–28. Leiden: Brill, 2013.

Scheid, John. *An Introduction to Roman Religion*. Translated by Janet Lloyd. Bloomington: Indiana University Press, 2003.

Schmidt, Francis. *How the Temple Thinks: Identity and Social Cohesion in Ancient Judaism*. The Biblical Seminar 78. Sheffield: Sheffield Academic Press, 2001.

Scott, James C. *Domination and the Arts of Resistance: Hidden Transcripts*. New Haven: Yale University Press, 1992.

Simundson, Daniel J. *The Book of Micah*. NIB 7. Nashville: Abingdon, 1996.

Silverstev, Alexei. "The Household Economy." In *The Oxford Handbook of Jewish Daily Life in Roman Palestine*, edited by Catherine Hezer, 230–44. Oxford: Oxford University Press, 2010.

Singer, Milton. *When a Great Tradition Modernizes: An Anthropological Approach to Indian Civilization*. New York: Praeger, 1972.

Ste. Croix, G. E. M. de. *The Class Struggle in the Ancient Greek World: From the Archaic Age to the Arab Conquests*. Ithaca, NY: Cornell University Press, 1980.

Tannehill, Robert C. *The Narrative Unity of Luke–Acts: A Literary Interpretation*. 2 vols. Minneapolis: Fortress Press, 1986, 1990.

Tuckman, B. W. "Developmental Sequence in Small Groups." *Psychological Bulletin* 63 (1965): 384–99.

Tyson, Joseph B. "The Birth Narratives and the Beginning of Luke's Gospel." *Semeia* 52 (1990): 103–20.

Wedgeworth, Steven. "The Meaning of the Magnificat." *Wedgeword* (blog). December 14, 2014. https://tinyurl.com/ycrmm74p.

Wenell, Karen J. "Contested Temple Space and Visionary Kingdom Space in Mark 11–12," *BibInt* 15 (2007): 323–37.

Wills, Lawrence M. *Not God's People: Insiders and Outsiders in the Biblical World*. New York: Rowman & Littlefield, 2008.

Wilson, Brittany E. *Unmanly Men: Refigurations of Masculinity in Luke–Acts*. Oxford: Oxford University Press, 2015.

Winn, Adam. *The Purpose of Mark's Gospel: An Early Christian Response to Roman Imperial Propaganda*. WUNT 245. Tübingen: Mohr Siebeck, 2008.

Wright, David. "Unclean and Clean (OT)." *ABD* 6 (1992): 729–41.

Wright, N. T. "Putting Paul Together Again: Toward a Synthesis of Paul's Theology." In *Paul's Theology: Volume 1, Thessalonians, Philippians, Galatians, Philemon*, edited by Jouette Basler, 183–211. Minneapolis: Fortress Press, 1991.

———. *The Resurrection of the Son of God*. Minneapolis: Fortress Press, 2003.

Zangenberg, Jürgen. "Pure Stone: Archaeological Evidence for Jewish Purity Practices in Late Second Temple Judaism (Miqwa'ot and Stone Vessels)." In *Purity and the Forming of Religious Traditions in the Ancient Mediterranean World and Ancient Judaism*, edited by Christian Frevel and Christophe Nihan, 537–72. Leiden: Brill, 2013.

Zias, Joseph. "Death and Disease in Ancient Israel." *Biblical Archaeologist* 54 (1991): 146–59.